Endangered Sky

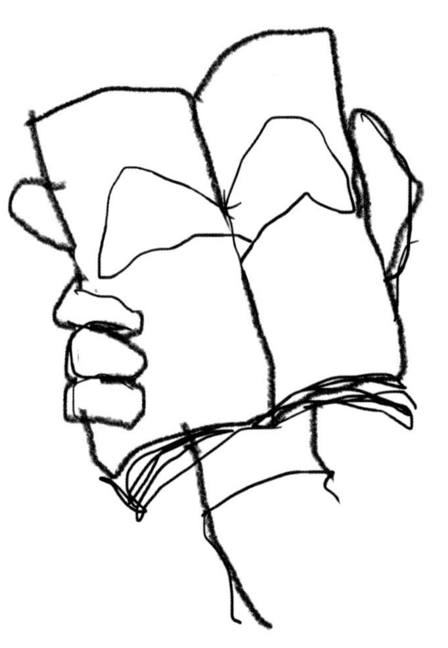

Endangered Sky

Sean Scully & Kelly Grovier

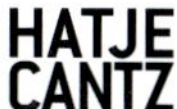

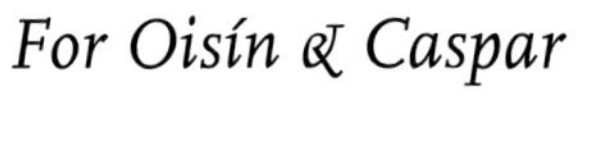

For Oisín & Caspar

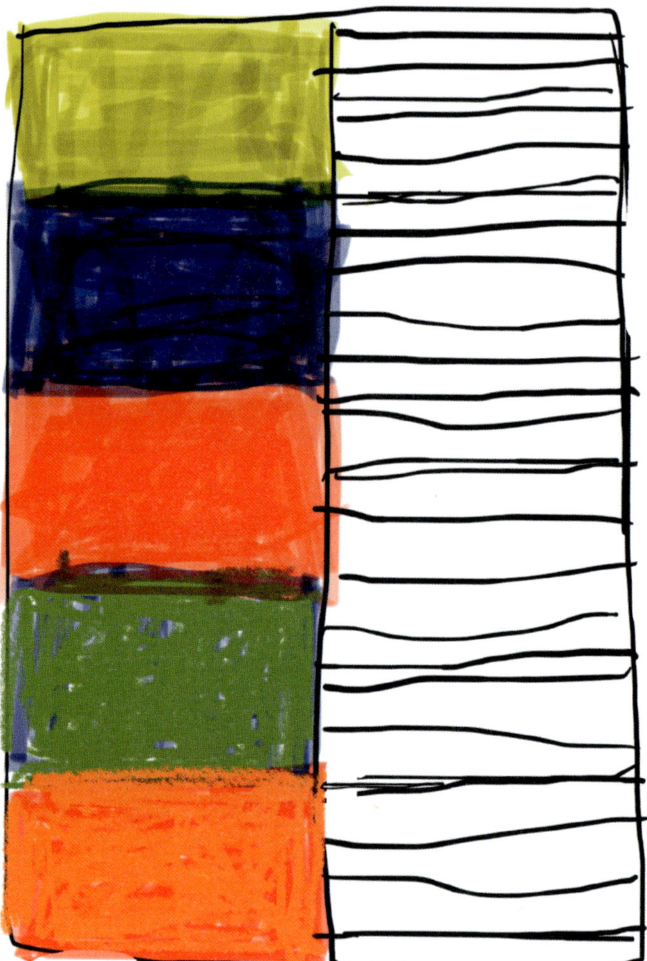

Table of Contents

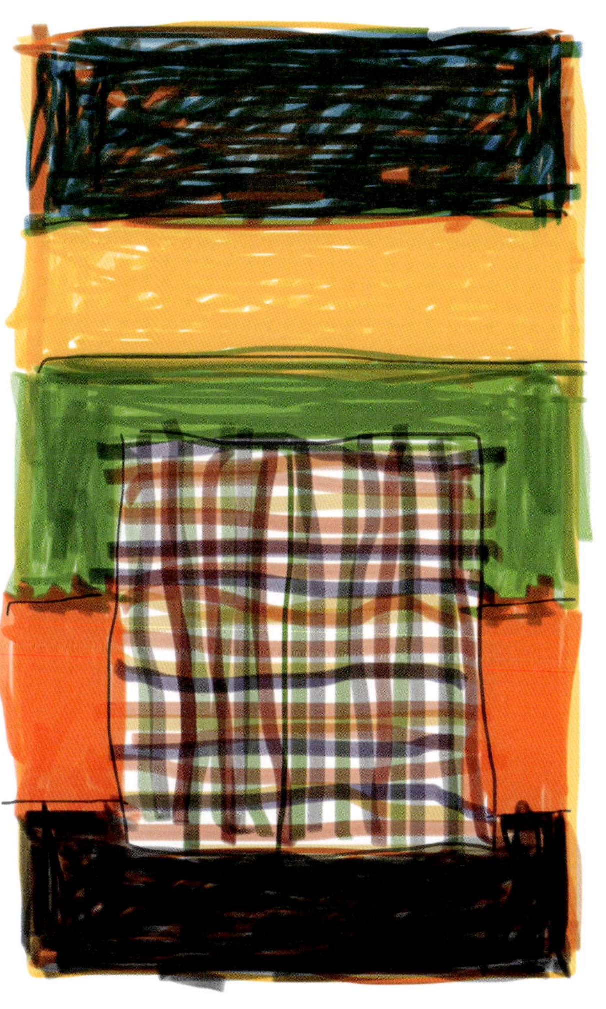

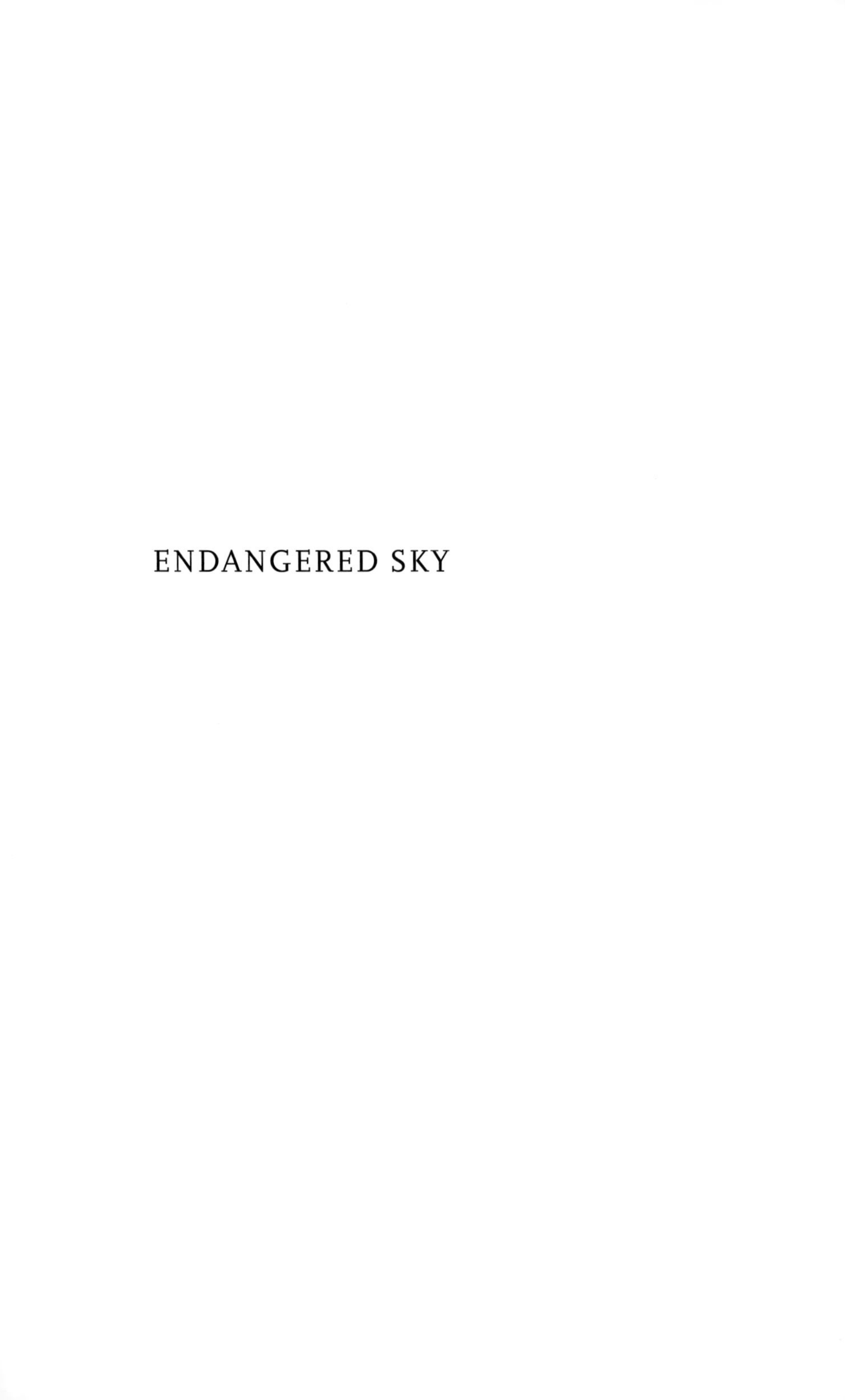

ENDANGERED SKY

In April 2021, while visiting the Bahamian island of
Eleuthera with his wife and son, Sean Scully began
drawing on his iPhone as he sat on a balcony, visited
by whispers of sea breeze and the bright flit and
chitter of bananaquits and red-legged thrushes – now
alighting, now winging away. The acclaimed abstract
artist soon found himself sketching with his fingertip
delicate grids of luminous colour that at once rhyme
with the rhythms of his famous large-scale oil paint-
ings and yet feel entirely new: fresh and impressionis-
tic geometries of intimate gesture as free as the air
of which they were born.

When Sean shared one of these new works (unaccom-
panied by any comment on its inception) with me
over email, I responded with a short poem likening
the evocative digital drawing – its electric greens and
phosphorescent yellows – to the plumage and plight
of the Sun Parakeet, an endangered South American
conure about which, by pure coincidence, I had just
been reading.

Immediately, Sean and I glimpsed in the synergy
of image and word an opportunity to meditate more
expansively, visually and verbally, on a crisis about
which we are both passionately concerned: the
vanishing beauty of the world's imperilled bird popu-
lation.

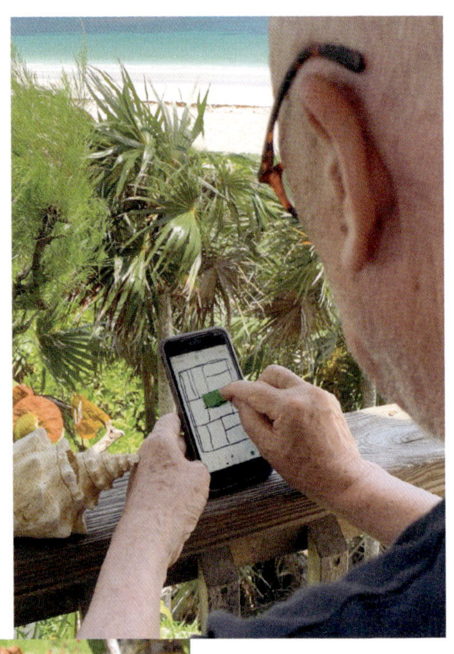

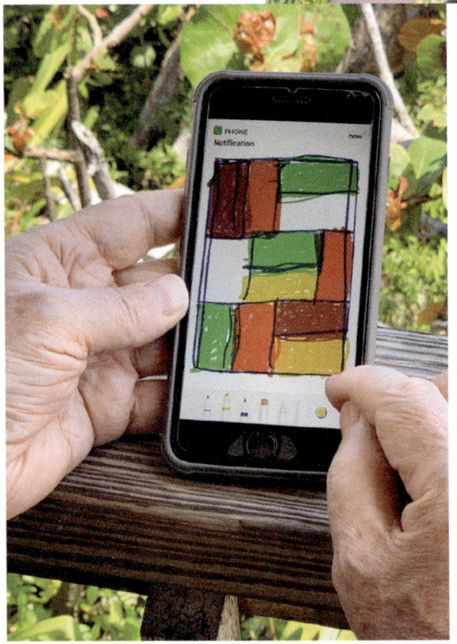
PHONE
now
Notification

It is estimated that as a result of climate change, illegal trade and habitat loss from the encroachments of technology and industrialisation, nearly half of the world's 11,000 species of birds are in decline and as many as 1 in 8 is heading towards global extinction.

Ever since Sean was a little boy growing up in South London, where he would nurse to health injured chicks in a makeshift clinic for sick animals that he operated from his family's home, he saw in the fragile freedom of birds, whose feathers brush the canvas of sky, a companionable form. Likewise, a key theme that runs through all of my collections of poems is an awe at the majesty of birds, from kingfishers to wrens, jackdaws to cockatoos.

Within days, Sean and I, from our far-flung perches in the Bahamas and Ireland (where I live with my wife and son), began to compile an aviary of conversing drawings and poems, each pairing devoted to the beauty and mystery of a single species of bird that is now under serious threat, if not already gone – from the New Caledonian Lorikeet to the Scarlet Honeycreeper, from the Chilean Woodstar to the Elfin Woods Warbler.

Sean's renowned visual language – at once calibrated and unchoreographed – is uniquely suited to capturing the essence of creatures that are, themselves, on the brink of becoming mere abstractions. His iPhone drawings are the ironic embodiment, he told me, of 'technology which is ruining nature turned inside out to protest its demise'. My poems, meanwhile, adhere to a fresh verse scheme I devised especially for *Endangered Sky*. Called an *alula*, after the ornithological term for the small group of feathers on a bird's wing that give it lift in flight, the stanza's five lines are distinguished by diminishing length from start to finish:

> *At first, the poem finds its wings, and then*
> *it scales the air. The next line's*
> *weightless, teasing forth*
> *a fifth not here*
> *nor there.*

The result is an informal form that accelerates and swoops – one whose shape mirrors the taper of an outstretched bird's wing. Taken together, these pairings of drawing and poem aim to offer something uplifting in the face of a preventable tragedy. 'Hope', after all, as Emily Dickinson famously wrote, 'is the thing with feathers / That perches in the soul.'

K. G.

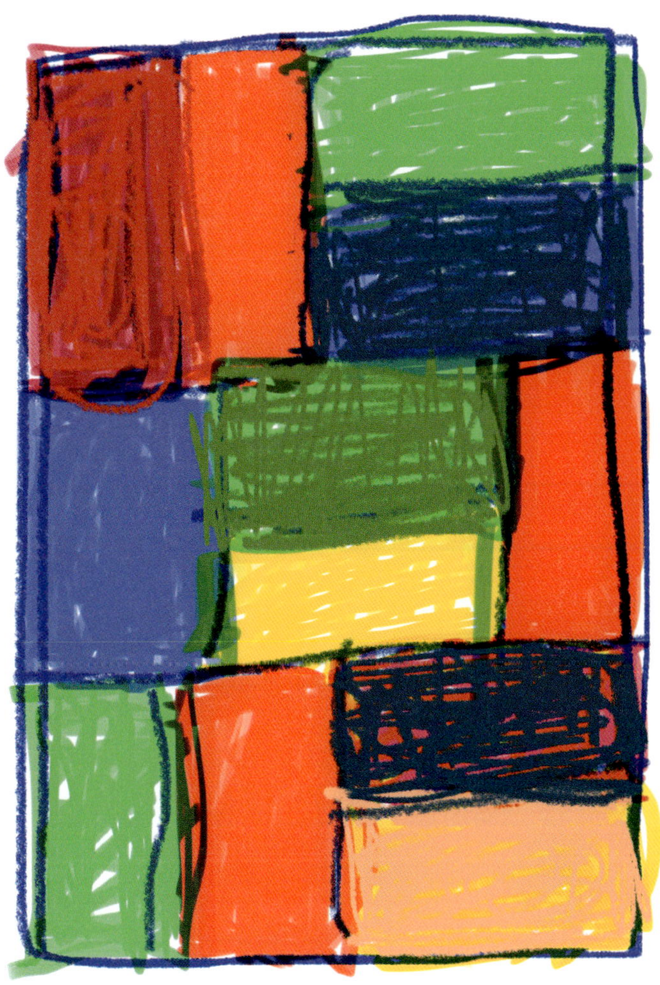

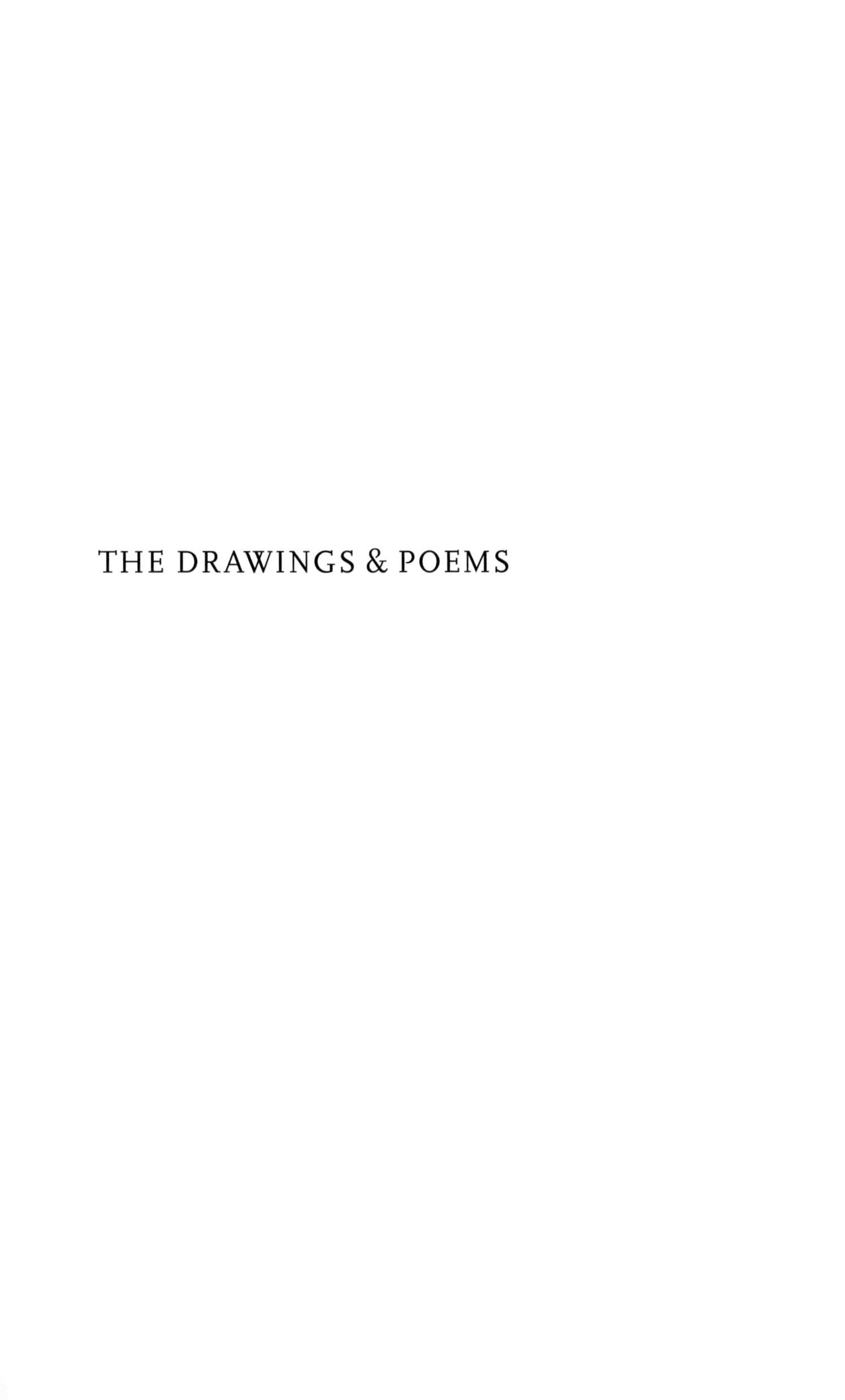

THE DRAWINGS & POEMS

Sun Parakeet

Status: 'Endangered' due to habitat loss

Into the ark of oblivion, one by one
we frogmarch nature –
the awkward strut
of the Great Auk,
the unseen

slip of the sea mink. Here,
the pixilated plumage
of the sun parakeet,
yellow-crowned,
jade-winged,

tail dipped in fire, stares at itself
in the deepening mirror
of nothingness while
all around,
the ship's

planks tremble between the silent
screech of colour and the lost
staccatos of a world
that used
to be.

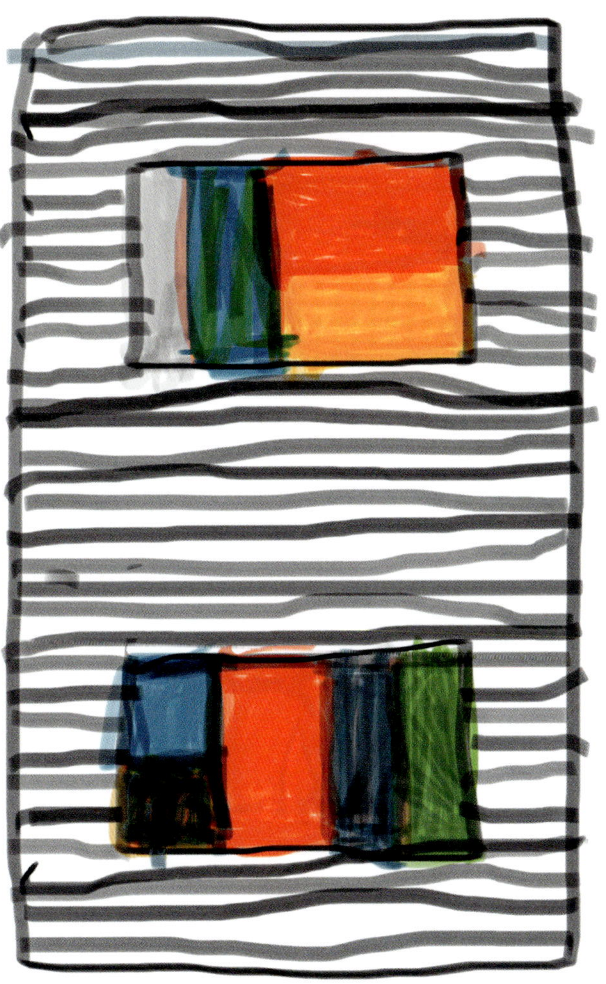

Little Forest Angel

Status: 'Vulnerable' due to deforestation
and cage-bird trading

Late one May or early one June,
I heard you calling *kwah-he,*
kwah-wu – way up, high
up on your slim tree
branch

not a worry or a care or a thing
to do, just whistle with
a wiggle of your
green-
tip

wing and your tail bright blue,
as the weary world waves
goodbye to you: *kwah-*
he, kwah-he, kwah-
wu.

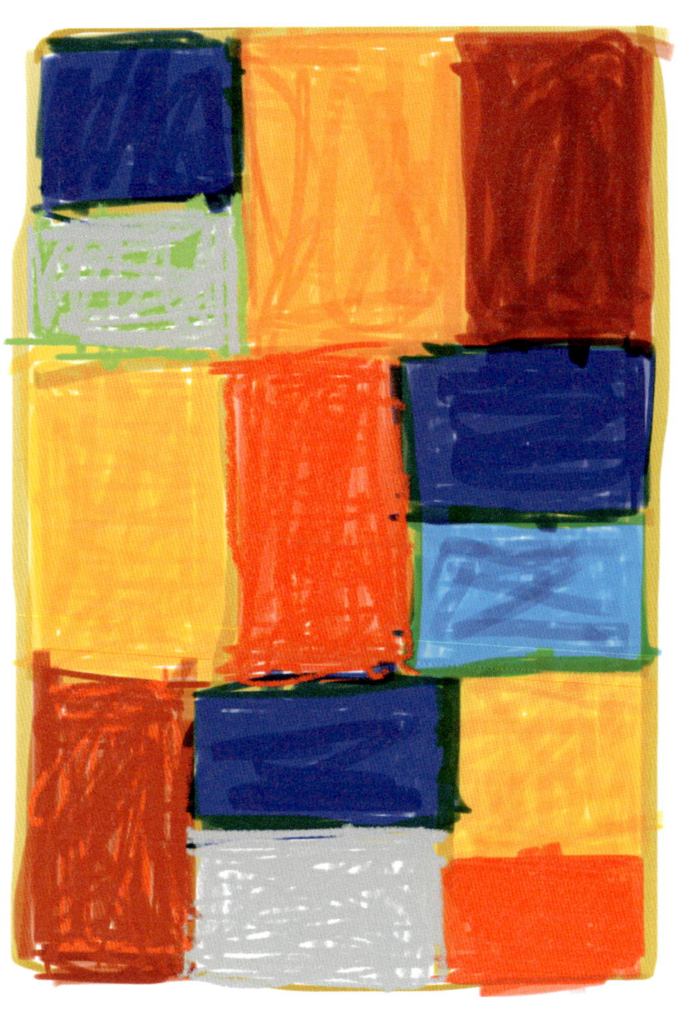

New Caledonian Lorikeet

Status: 'Critically endangered'; last spotted in 1987

If death is never truly loss but mere
dispersal, a slow exchange
of self for immensity
of infusion, we
will find

your jade wings not in the fans of fish-
bone ferns but echoes of viridian
light glinting from the forest,
see your scarlet
beak

in the pink petals of puckered dusk, hear
your sapphire crown still humming
in the silent hymns
of the morning
mist.

Kākāpō

Status: 'Critically endangered' due to habitat loss

No wonder they took you
for a prophet, sooth-
saying in the secret
shade of the rumi,
shuffling

your scruff of sage feathers
in serious soil as you
scryed the black
berries of the
tawa tree

like tea leaves – the knowing
swirl of your owlish, moon-
dial head. But if it's so,
tell me, beady-eyed
big foot,

two talons pointing to
eclipse, how on
earth is it you
never saw us
coming?

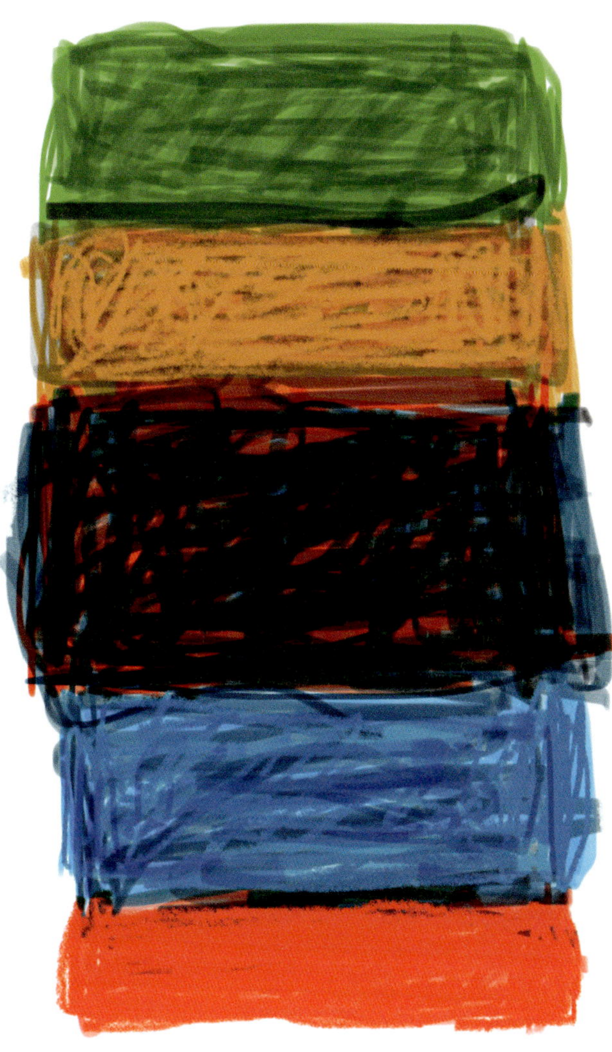

Resplendent Quetzal

Status: 'Near threatened' due to habitat loss

Like the robin, who seared his throat
rust red ripping thorns
from the weeping
brow of
Christ,

you too know something about
death – swooping to souse
your breast in the blood
of Mayan kings –
know

about the loss of self
and song – the dark
iridescence
of the
soul.

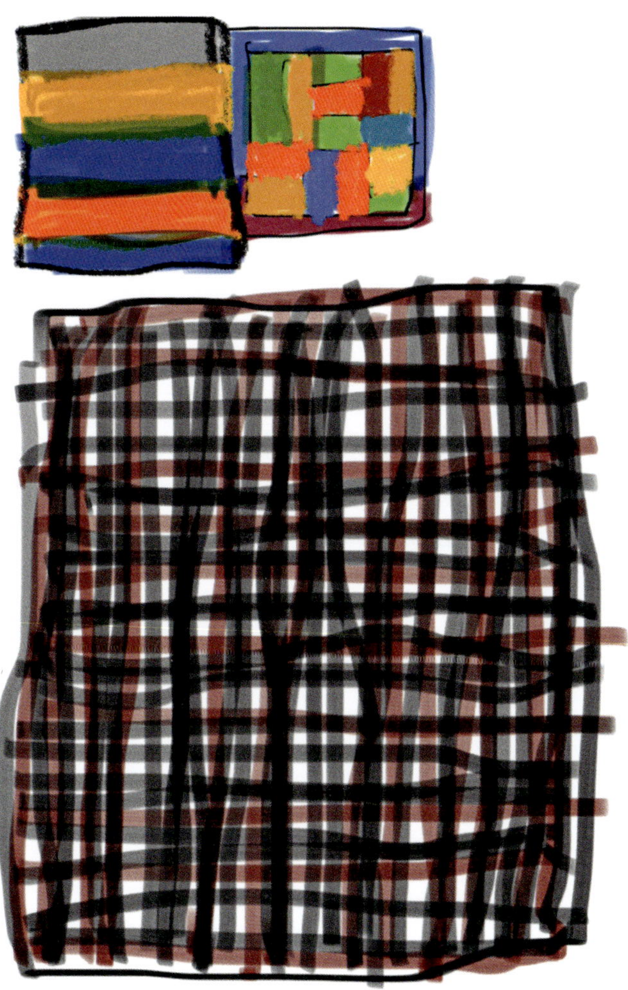

Red-and-Blue Lory

Status: 'Endangered' due to illegal trapping,
pet trade and insecticide use

That you were ever other than a fable –
a fanciful fusion of fire and ice,
of sunrise red and midnight
blue – is the real miracle
of your being. Prone

to ruffled dashes where the black birdwing
butterfly swoops, your fitful sprints blur
the line between a world that isn't
and one that can never
be again.

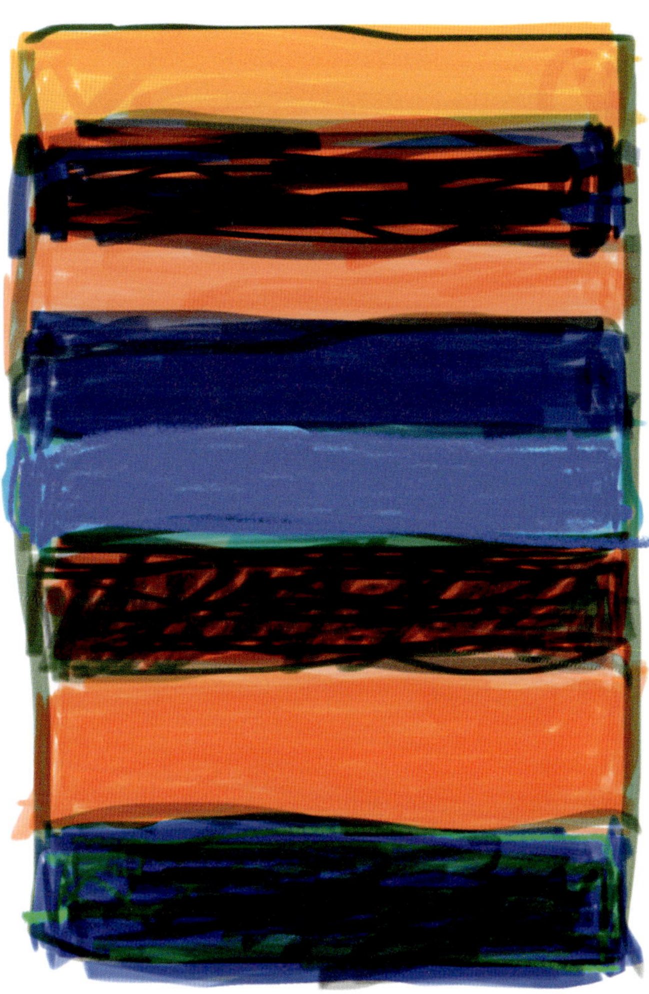

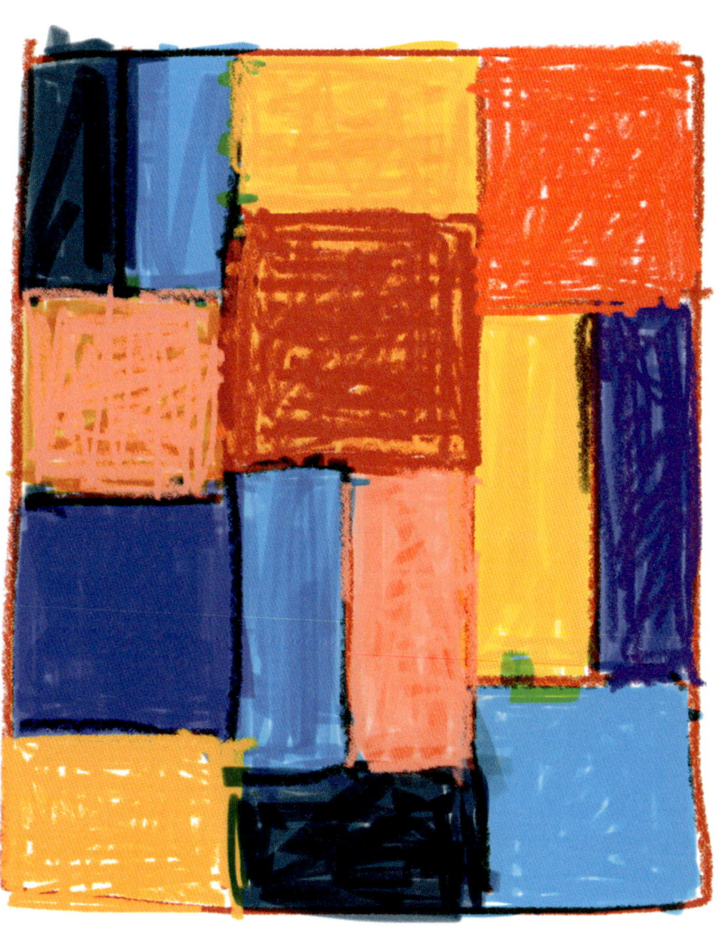

Scarlet Honeycreeper

Status: 'Vulnerable' due to habitat loss

As if your grapnel beak
has jimmied a door
to the invisible,
your song is
a rusted

hinge – a creak echoing
from the indigo
bellflowers
of no-
where.

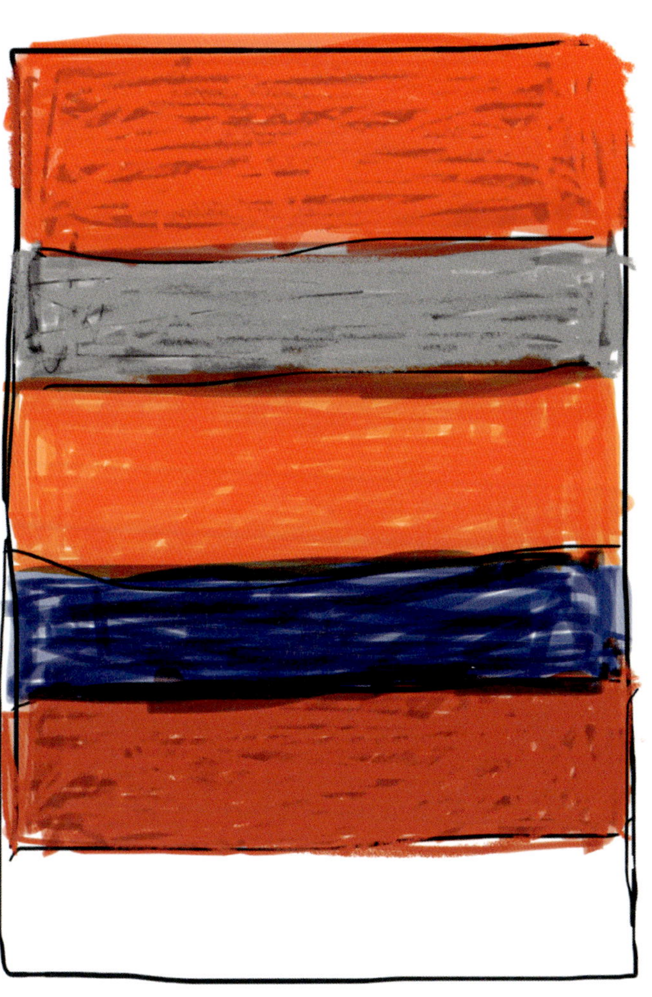

Stresemann's Bristlefront

*Status: 'Critically endangered'; one known
in existence*

A deceleration is gathering, a sift
of deciduous light, as the last
burnished blue prickle
of crown dandles
down

to rest, and, as it eases, scratches
the canopied air, adding one
more invisible tick to our
cruel, imperishable
tally.

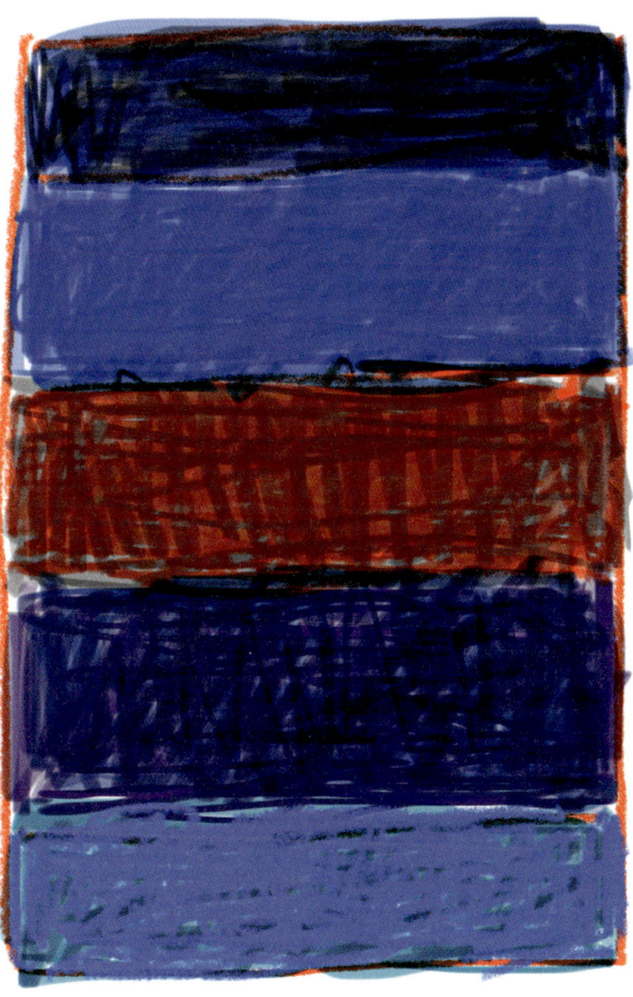

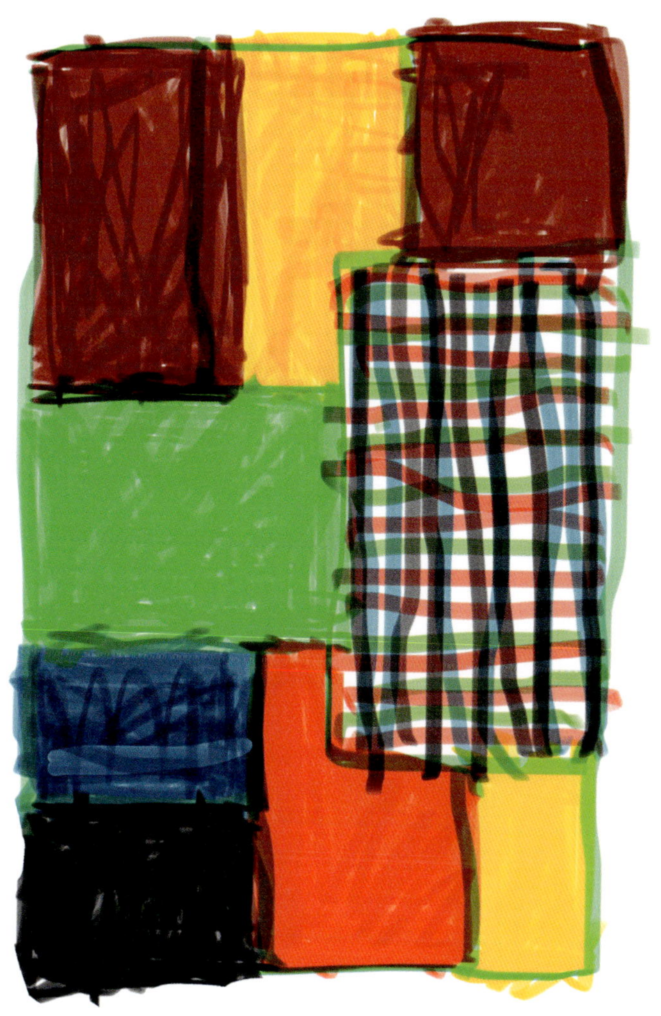

Starling

Status: 89% decline in the UK since 1969

Starling wing on the mistblue lawn—
applepetal pink, pink sky gone—
God of souldusk, purplemoon
glows, so strange the way
world comes

and goes.

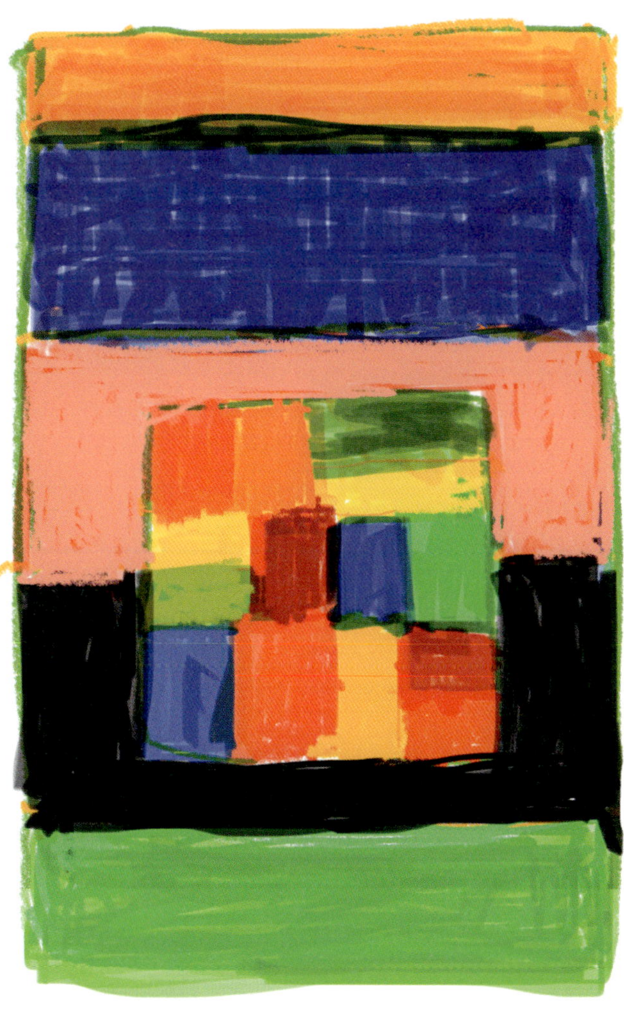

Chilean Woodstar

Status: 'Critically endangered' due to habitat loss

Hover of purple throat and whittled bill
tilting below a smudge of smoked
agave, your heart, punching
above its weightlessness,
splices the world

into a shiver of luminous slides –
orpiment sunset and rush
of river blue. You always
were more motion
than muscle,

more flit than feather. Now,
the shadow you were
never still enough to
cast is catching
up with you,

whistling its hollow
symphony through
your vanishing
pan flute of
bones.

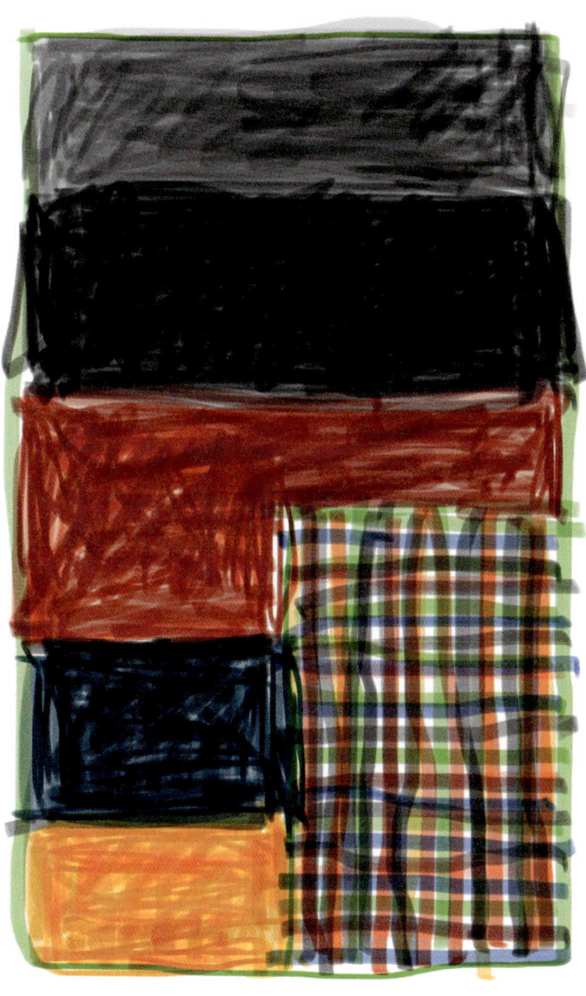

Black Robin

*Status: 'Endangered' due to habitat loss
and nest predation*

Dusky dawnlight. Deafening quiet.
No notes, just ghosts,
where nests wove
riot. No *chirr-*
chirr-chip;

no *cheep-cheep-chirr.*
Just blankness
where once
blackness
stirred.

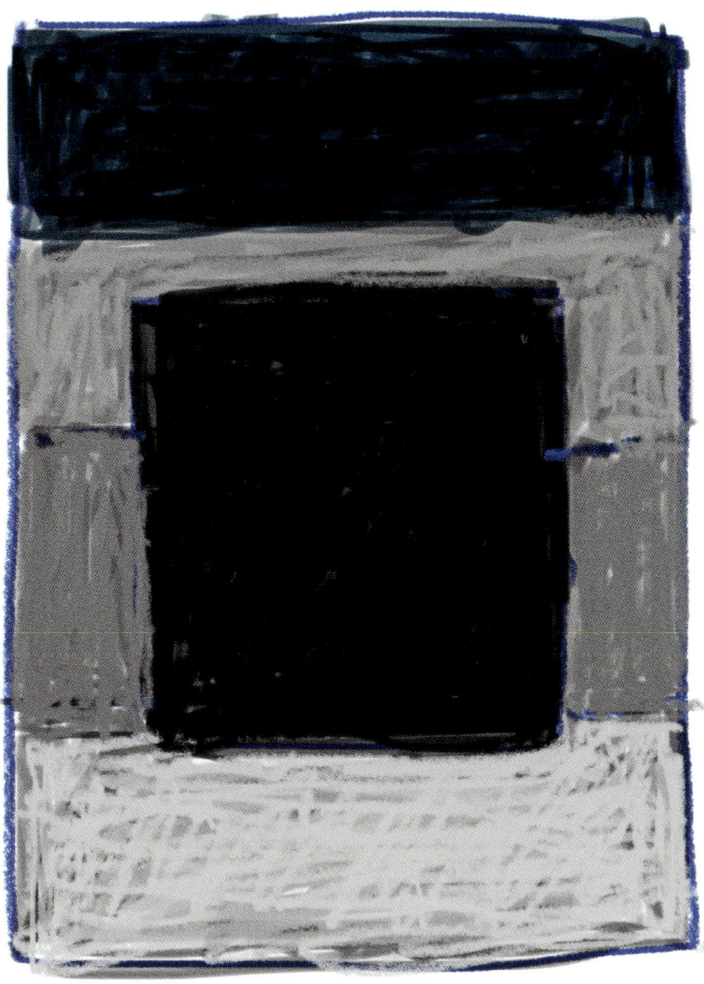

Red-Throated Lorikeet

Status: 'Critically endangered'; last recorded in 1993

Every minute, your fluorescent feathers fade
deeper into myth, merge with the mind
of the snake-neck Hō-ō, the dark
caw of the Hakawai.
I wonder

who it was that spied you last as you
melted into memory behind
hemlock – a flying fox,
perhaps, or tine-
tailed emperor,

skewing its chrysalis – its new
eyes awing at the immortal
splendour of your
snuffed-out
grace.

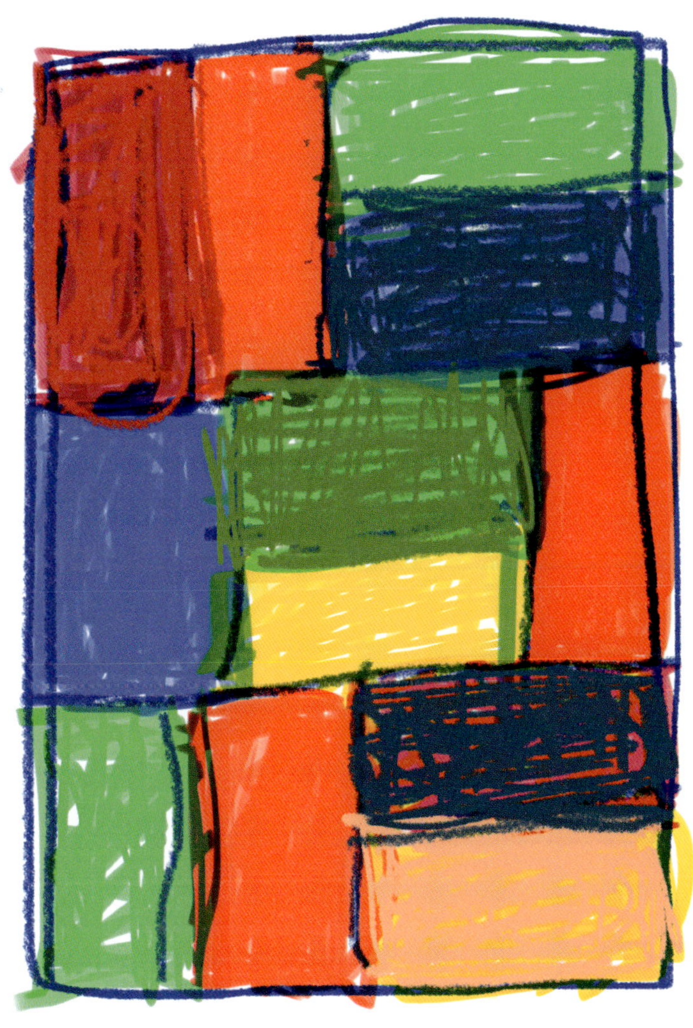

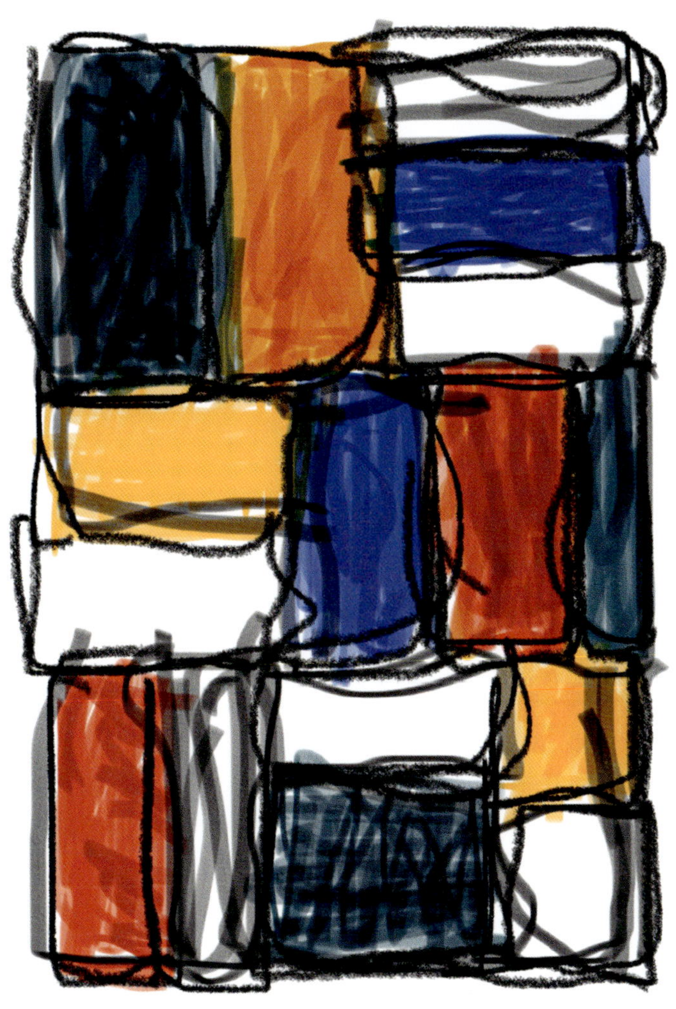

Hawai'i 'akepa

Status: 'Endangered'; existence confined to one island

You're never mentioned in the island legend
of the jealous goddess Pele, who turned
the dashing warrior 'Ōhi'a into a tree
for scorning her advances.
And then,

in a fit of spiteful pity, crushed his heart-
sick lover, Lehua, to a fist of fiery
quills that quiver forever
on his branches.
Yet it's you

who keeps their love burning, crossbilled
flicker of orange, trilling their soft
sweet nothings as you flit
from ear to trembling
ear.

Cuban Macaw

56

Fire-fangled like a phoenix – blood-winged,
burning, you've mastered the mystery
of rainbows unweaving –
ghost of colour,
ash of air.

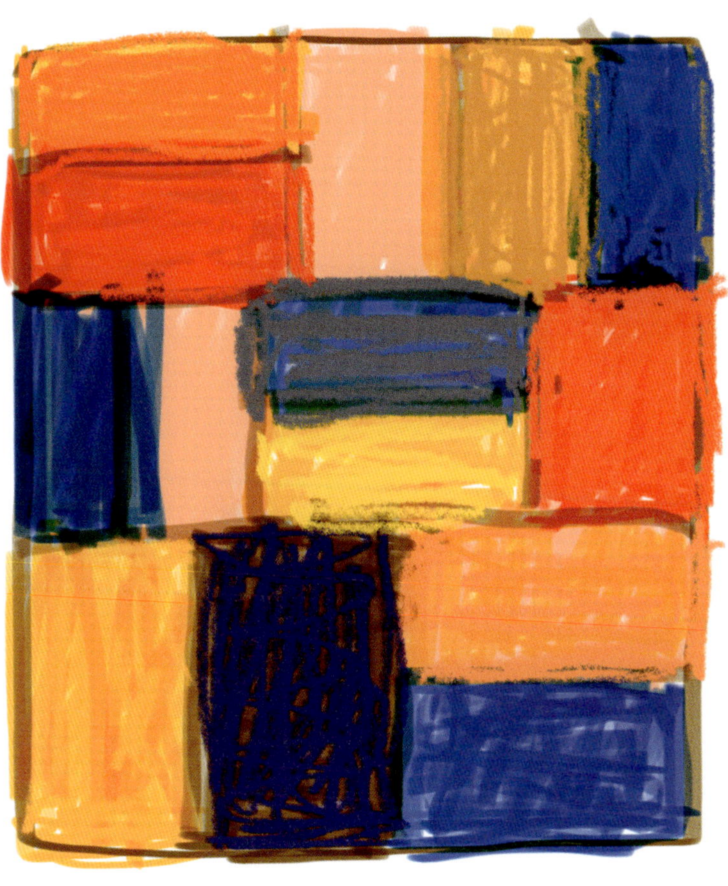

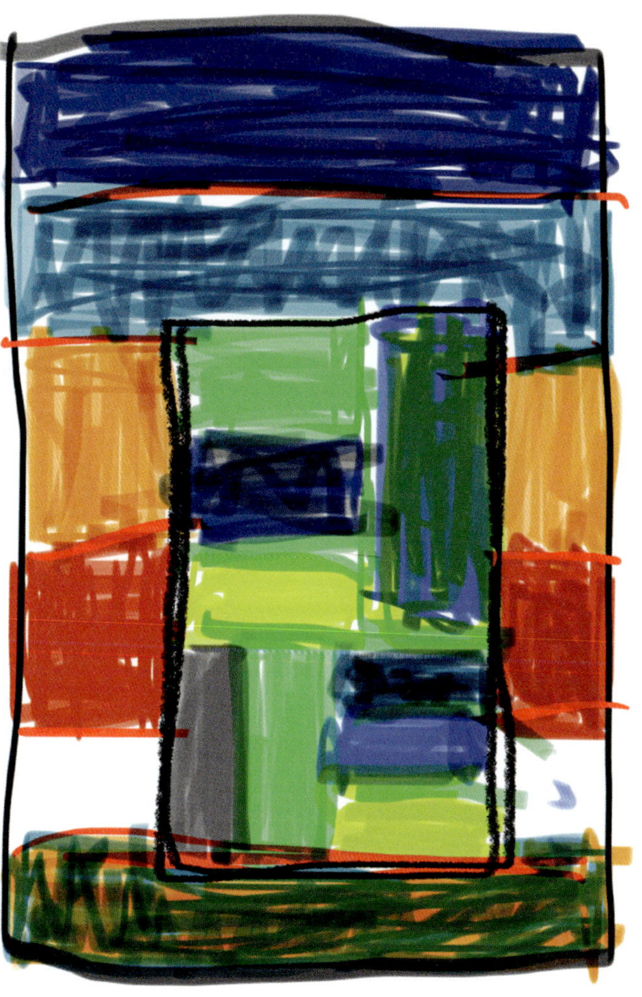

Secretarybird

Hawk-headed heron; morning-suited snake-
strangler; raptor-toed throwback
to the terror of Troodons
and Archaeopteryx;
you who

woo the air with dark pendulous plummets
and hustle the lizard-lurking shadows
of the humid savannah like long-
legged death, who knew
the next name

nibbed in your little black book –
the soul you'd find
yourself stalking –
would be
you?

Juan Fernández Firecrown

Status: 'Critically endangered' due to habitat loss

With the clout and lock-eyed fix
of a falcon and the sharp
citrus poise of orioles
so far outside
my grasp,

I set my sights instead on you,
firecrown – on your awk-
ward, tail-turvy
cling to the
tassels

of the cabbage tree flower, the way
you flip the world upside down,
fluting nectar, and bury
your beak deep
into now.

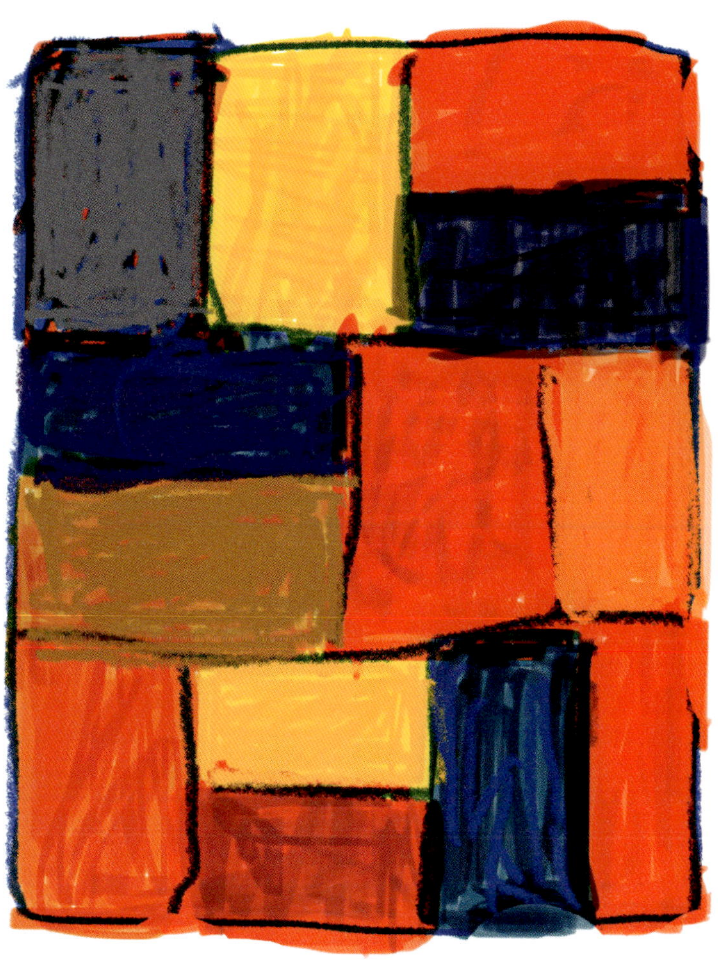

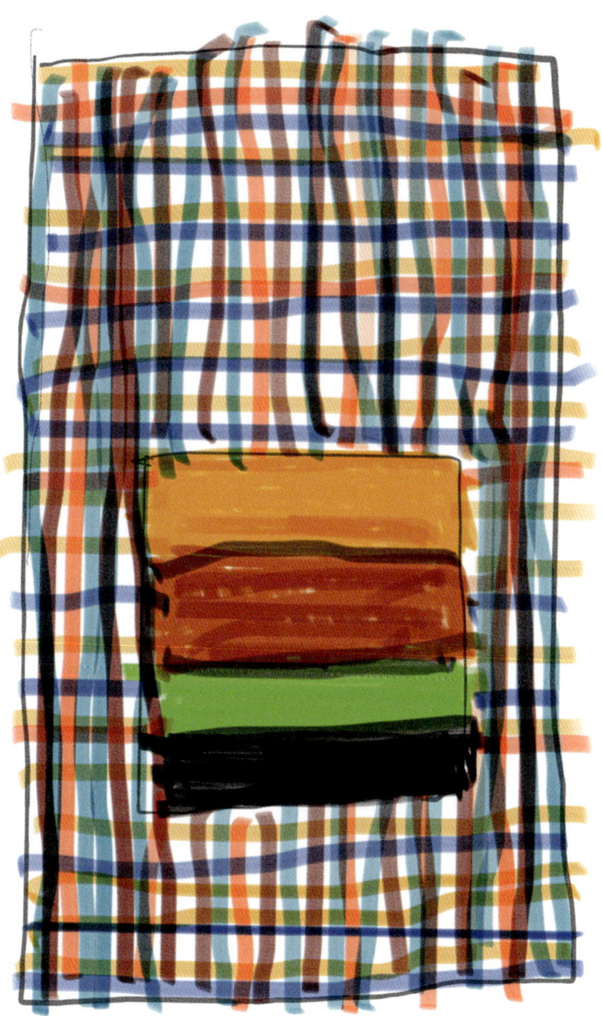

Crested Ibis

Status: 'Endangered' due to ongoing habitat loss

Watching you lumber from your needled
roost, high above this frog-sprung cove,
wobbling the pine as you clamber
air, ghost-gowned, blood-
faced, parting

the rain's beaded curtain with the tip
of your crowbar beak, I wonder
what it is, my friend, you and I
can ever really know
about death.

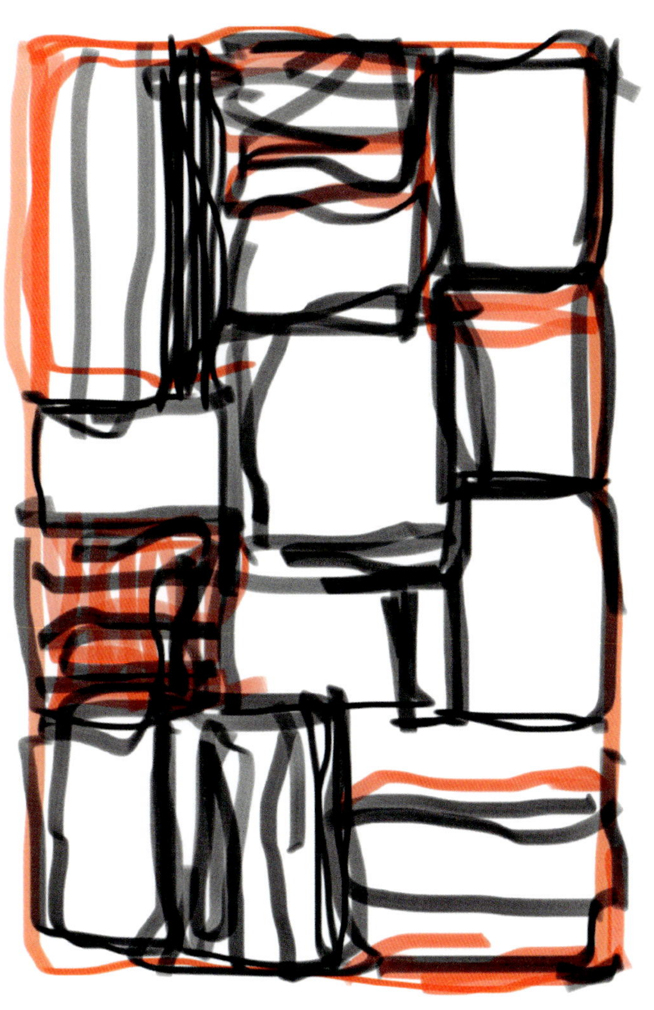

Elfin Woods Warbler

*Status: Discovered in Puerto Rico in 1968;
'endangered' due to habitat destruction*

Spirit of the disappearing forest,
your dappled feathers echo
the fractured light
of the canopy
like words

scribbled on a living page, crossed
out by shadows – a poem
forever unfinished –
can never be
erased.

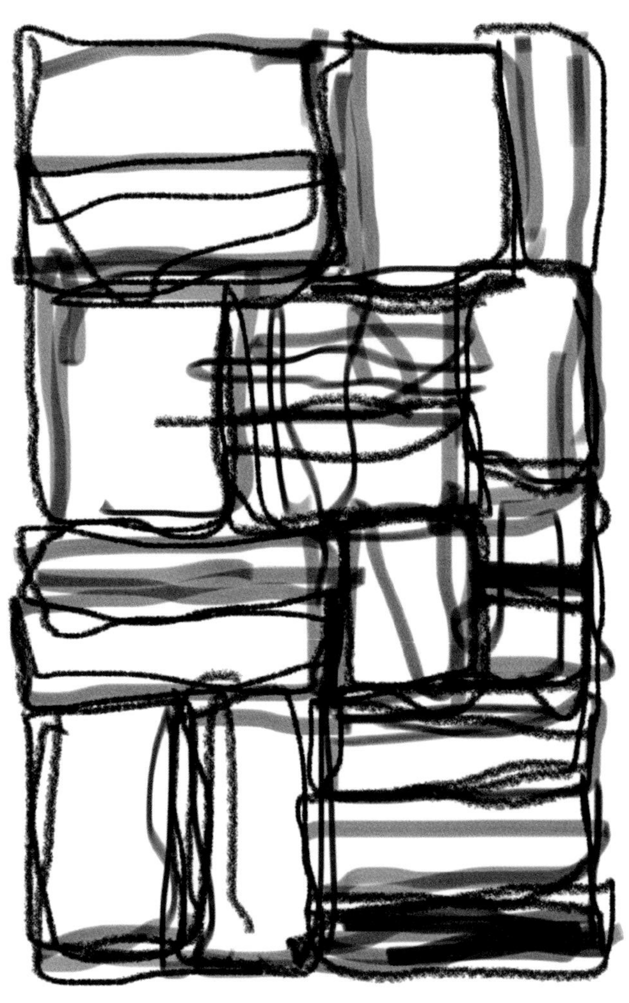

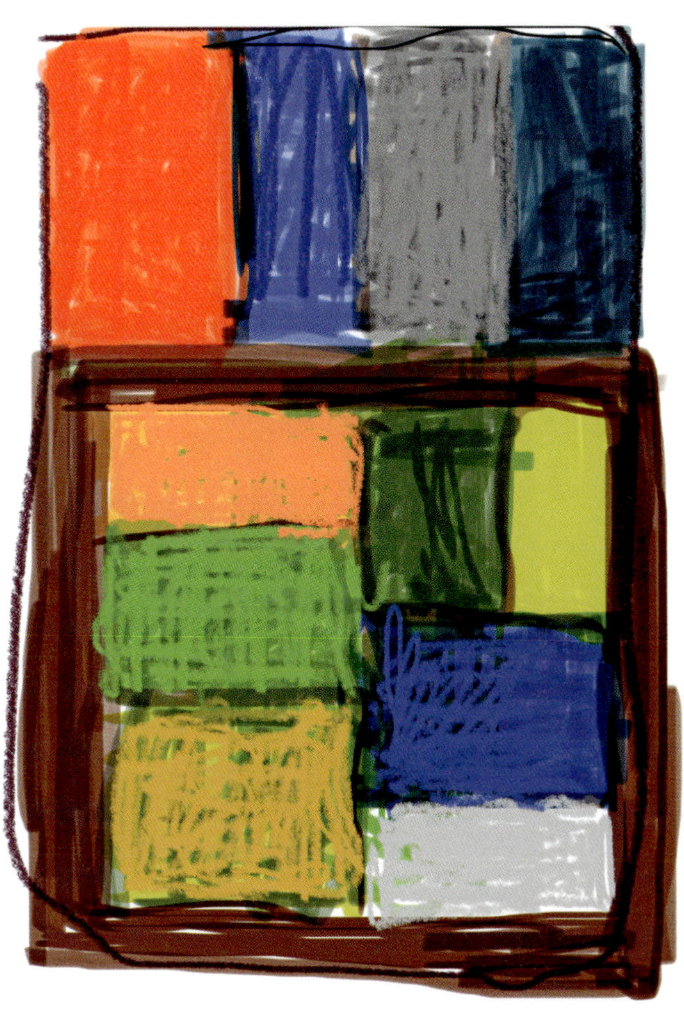

Javan Green Magpie

*Status: 'Critically endangered' due to habitat loss
and illegal trade; may be extinct in the wild*

Like a stack of stacking dolls, your heart's song
is caged in the cage of my singing heart.
A nest of souls, the more we are
stripped away, the more
we are one.

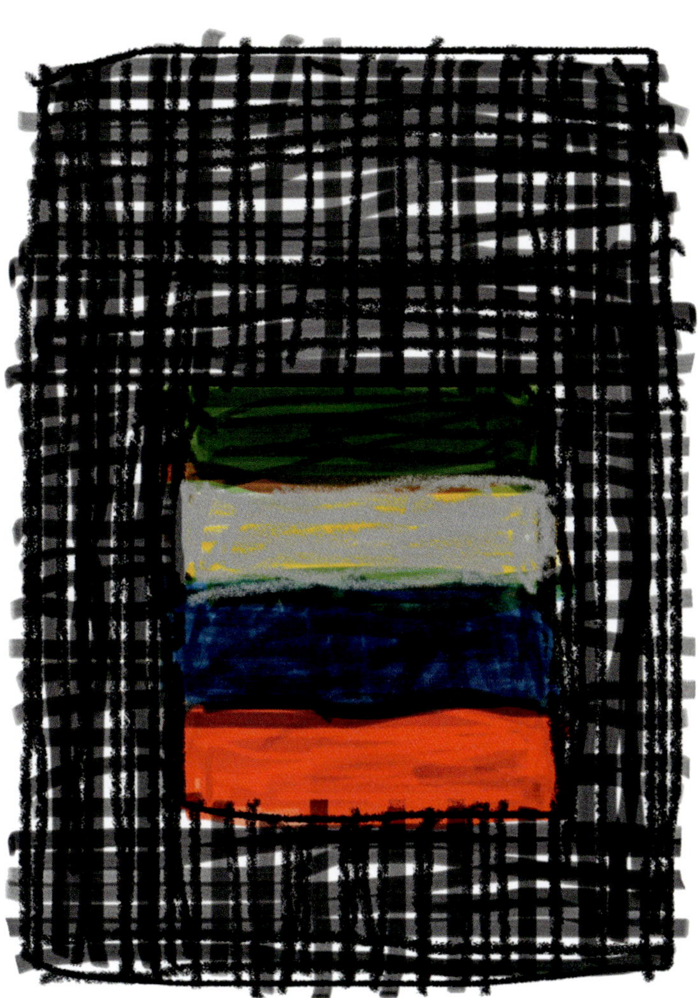

Blue-Banded Kingfisher

Status: 'Critically endangered'

Every time you take your harpoon
plunge – whetted beak breaking
the still glass of time, furrows
feathering out, bending
light to brilliant

wave as you buckle the river's
respirations – heart holds
its brittle breath
and braces for
the surge.

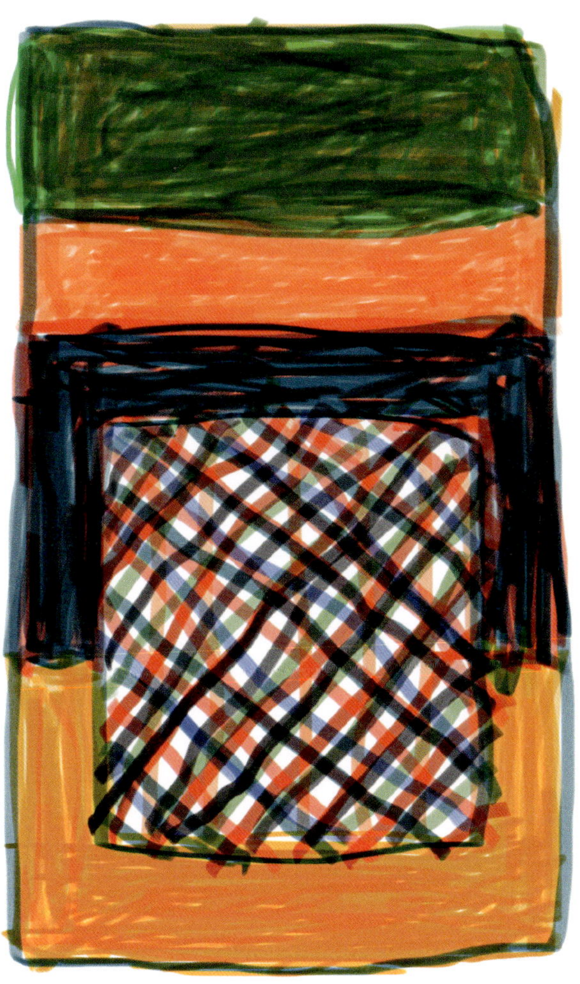

Rufous Hummingbird

*Status: 'Near threatened' due to climate change,
pesticides and global decline in insect populations*

Because the earth's watch
is running fast, because
we've jammed its
jewels, your
lagging

heart is falling out of sync
with the bees' thrum,
the pointless aim
of the flowers'
pistil.

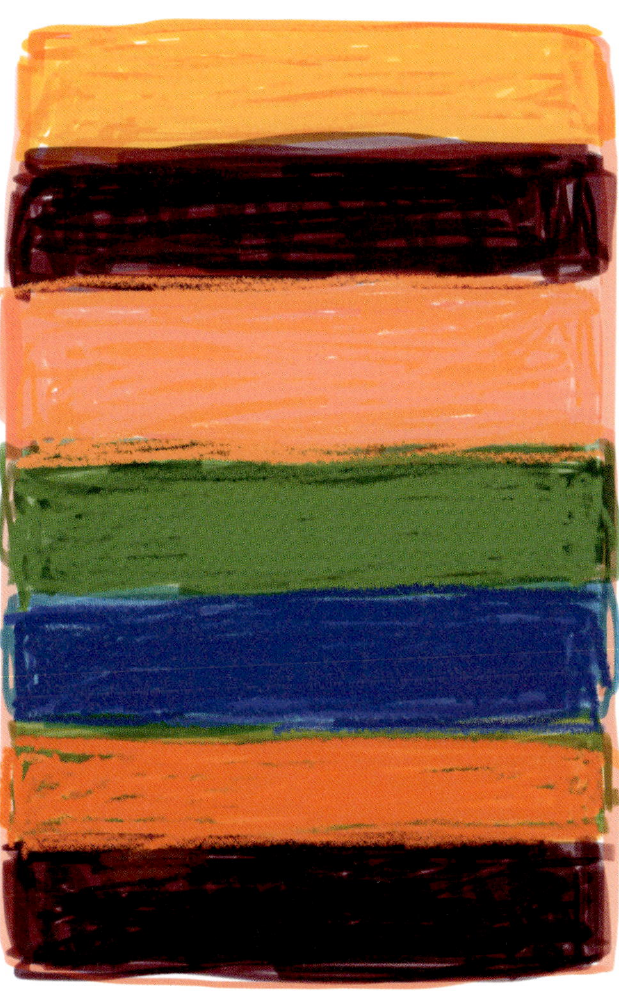

Pernambuco Pygmy Owl

*Status: 'Critically endangered' due to almost
complete destruction of habitat; unseen since 2001*

My head spins at your spinning
head – your orbits of mind
and ambits of thought –
how your eye-
shine turns

the night to thermal symphonies
of clicking tymbals, twists
the darkness
to focused
blur.

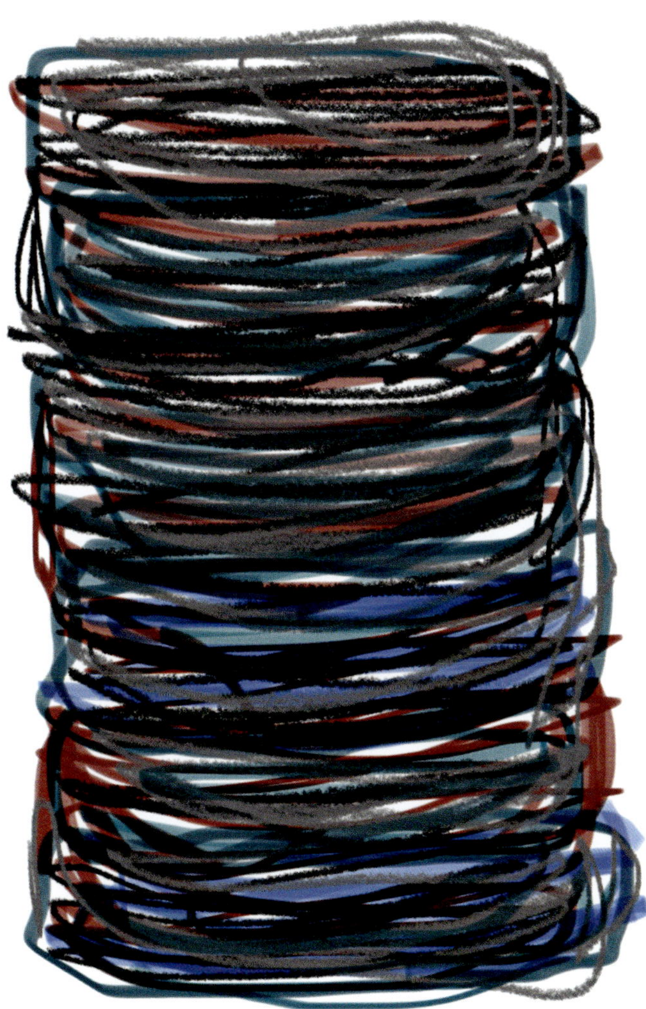

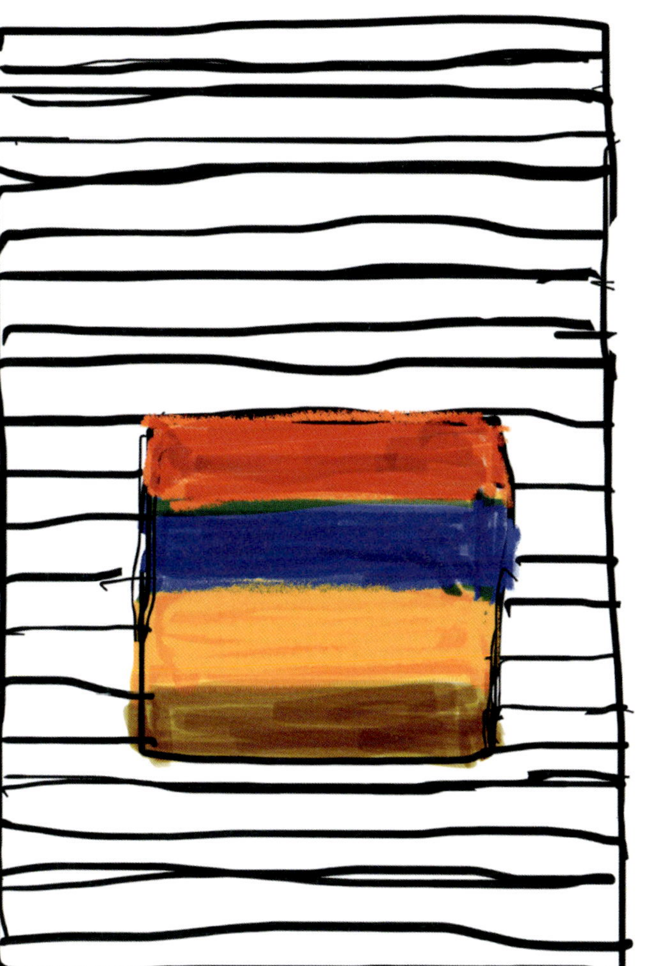

Passenger Pigeon

Here we are again, nodding past each other
along the long ledge, waiting
for a hand to reach out
and throw us a few
crumbs.

At a certain hour, when the sky
thickens and this pane
deepens to a mirror,
we will know
it's time

to take flight, to feather the air
above the city's slow ignition
of stars, to dazzle the dark
iridescent into
nothing.

Magenta Petrel

*Status: 'Critically endangered'; 80% population
decline in 60 years*

Weird the way world pulls us
inside out – a body
rising slowly
from its
soul:

sea from mind and mind
that syncs with sea.
It's only blankness
knows what
it's about –

emptiness alone is wholly
whole – and being
not in time
will be
to be.

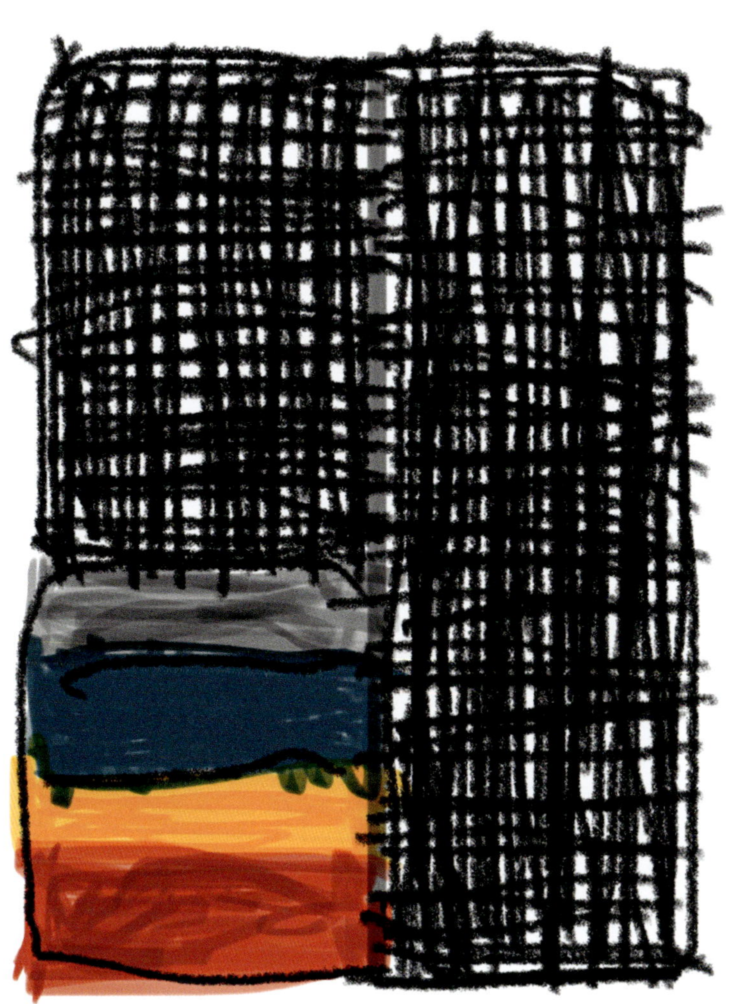

Kagu

*Status: 'Endangered'; population long in decline
from trapping for trade and non-native predators*

Bloodshot ghost of the forest floor,
powder-plumed and flightless,
how long have you stalked
these muggy shadows,
stood there

stilted on one smouldering leg waiting
for the acid soil to rumple, before
your beak bolted and you
snipped me
in two?

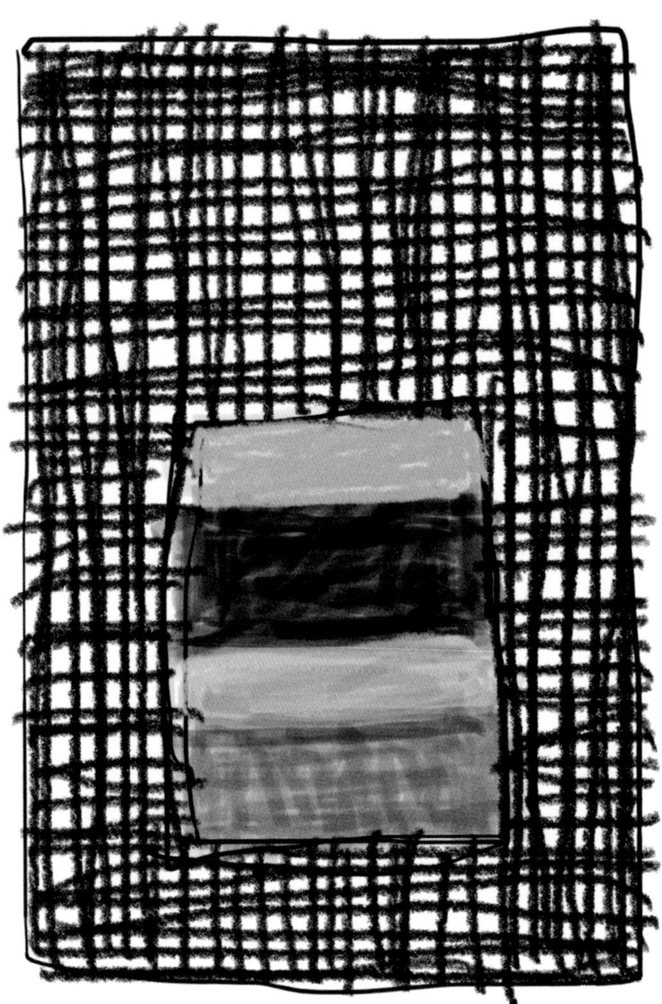

Red-Crowned Crane

Status: 'Vulnerable' due to habitat loss

Ruffling the lilac light, the soul
is stranger here – we sync
our song to rush of stars,
white wings to frost-
moon air.

Across the deepening dusk-
glow, our ink tail feathers
jot – a shadow scrawl,
a mist-hung hymn –
a poet's parting

shot.

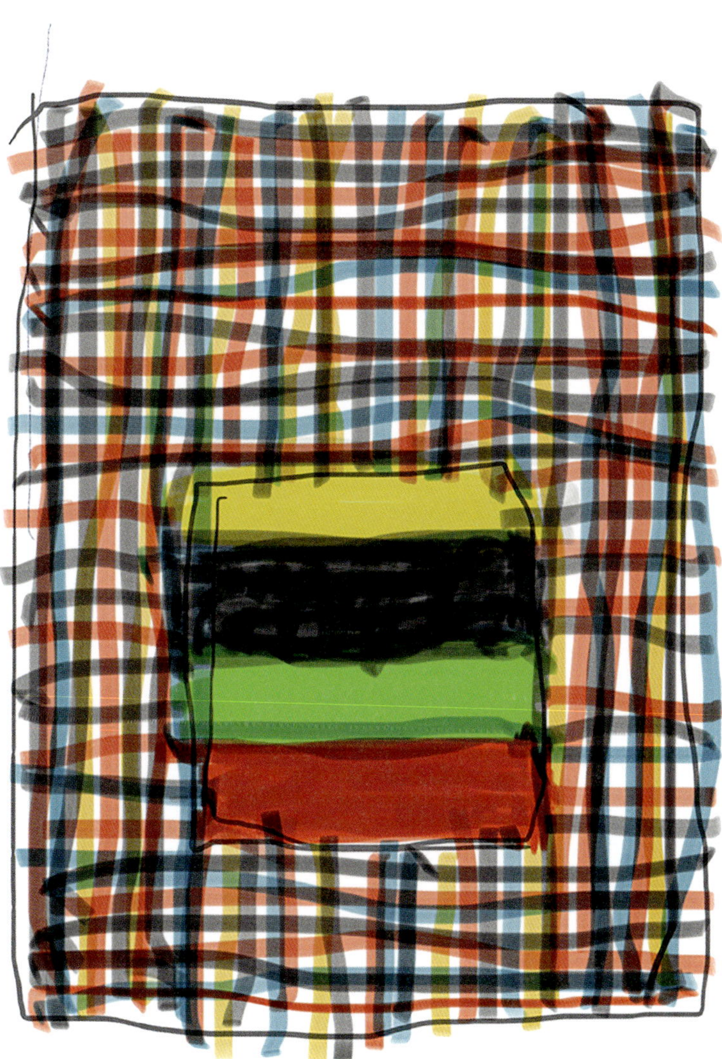

African Grey Parrot

Status: 'Endangered' due to trapping,
trade and use in traditional medicine

Mimicking the hawk's husky cry
and the falcon's harsh *kawk-*
kawk-kawk, you threw
the palm tree
vulture

off your scent, hid your flicker of tail
feathers behind a forest veil
of counterfeit calls.
But your grift
of gab

is now the cage in which you disappear,
mugging for a pinch of seed, aping
those who crave nothing but
echoes of their own
vanishing.

Sangihe Dwarf-Kingfisher

*Status: 'Critically endangered' if not extinct;
not seen since 1997*

I can almost feel your eye
swivel in the weave
of shadow-branch
just beyond
the edge

of thought, sense your vermillion
mind oscillate beneath
the warp and weft
of the river's
fluid

tapestry, and hear the quickening
pitch of your peach heart,
blue tail twitching,
your fiery beak
steeling

for the shred.

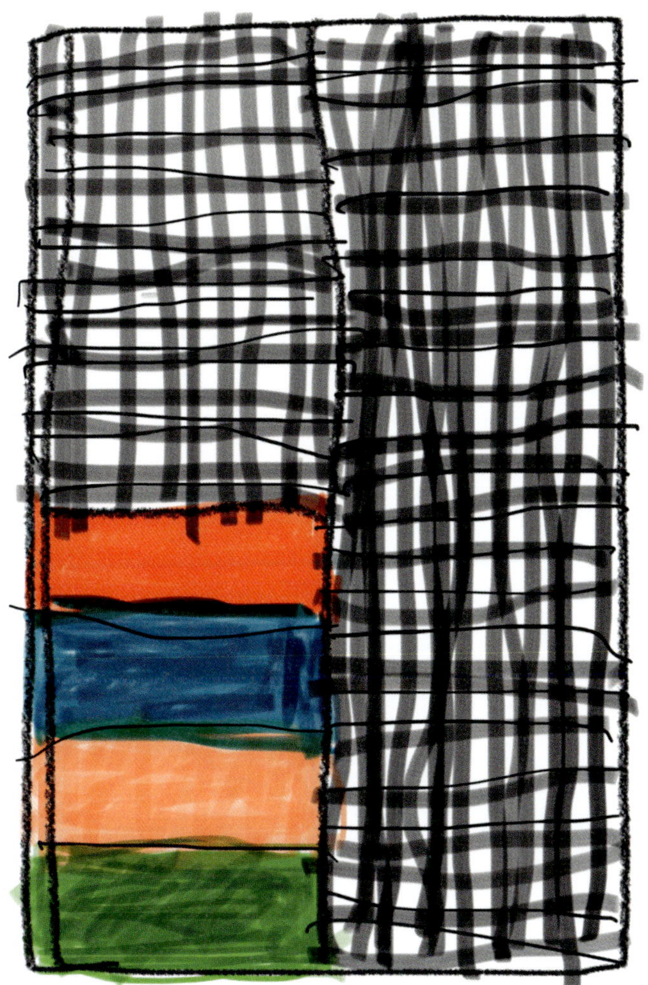

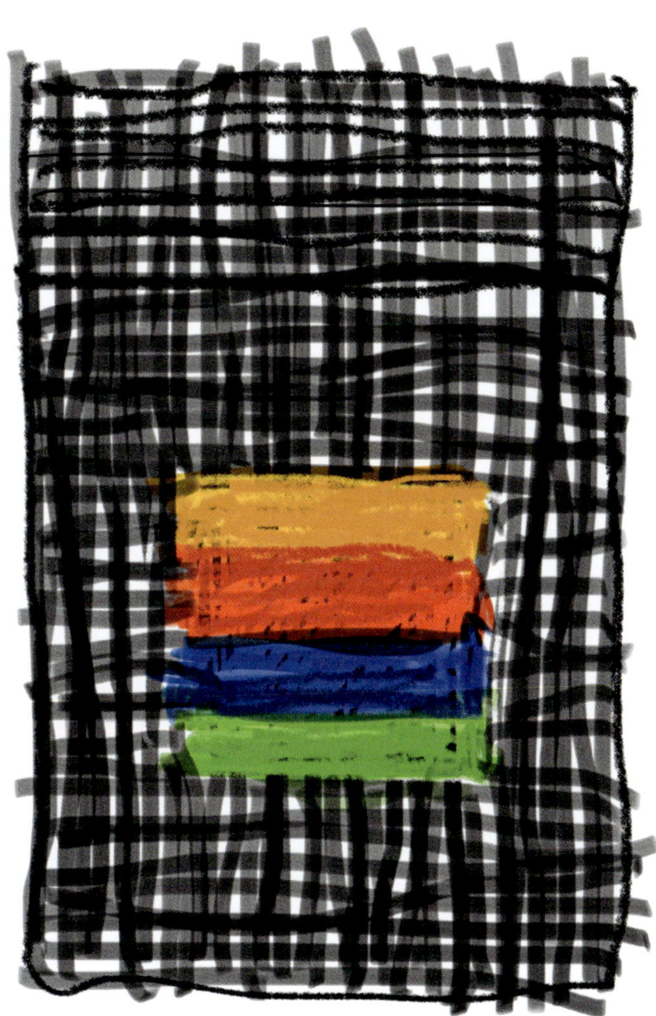

Black-Winged Lory

Status: 'Near threatened' due to habitat loss

Synapse snaps in the high tree brain,
your black wings flap and flap
again. World is dream –
a flash, a flutter;
leaves,

like eyelids, twitch and judder.
The tree's now empty, waves
gone flat – no colour,
call – and that
is that.

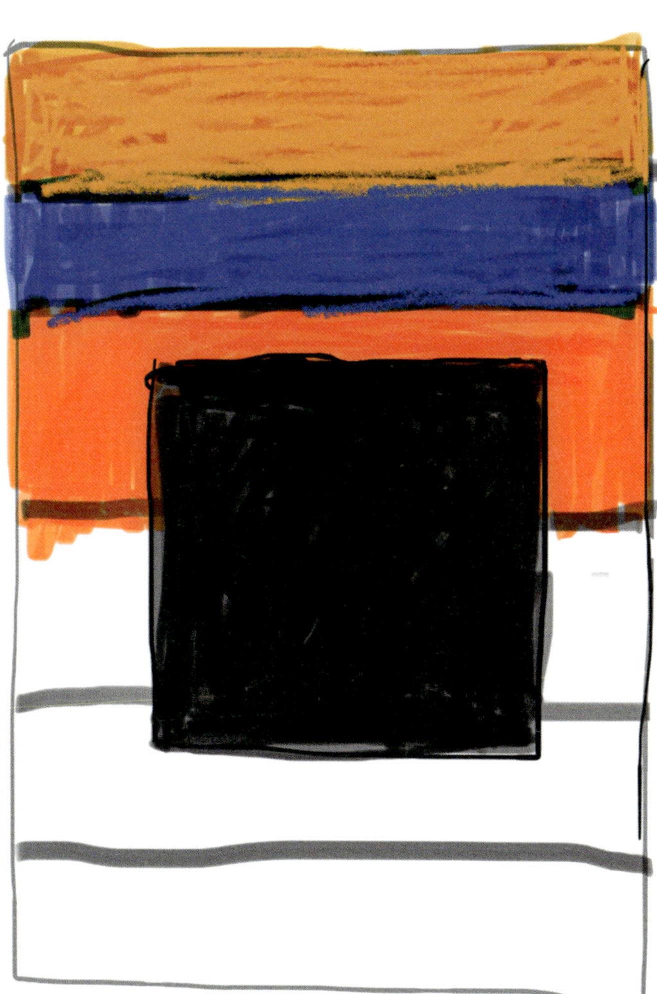

Wilson's Bird of Paradise

*Status: 'Near threatened' due to habitat loss,
limited range and exploitation*

Suddenly, inside the soul – a fire dance
of forest feather – jabber of green
and talons blue – flitters
the fleeting heart
and is gone.

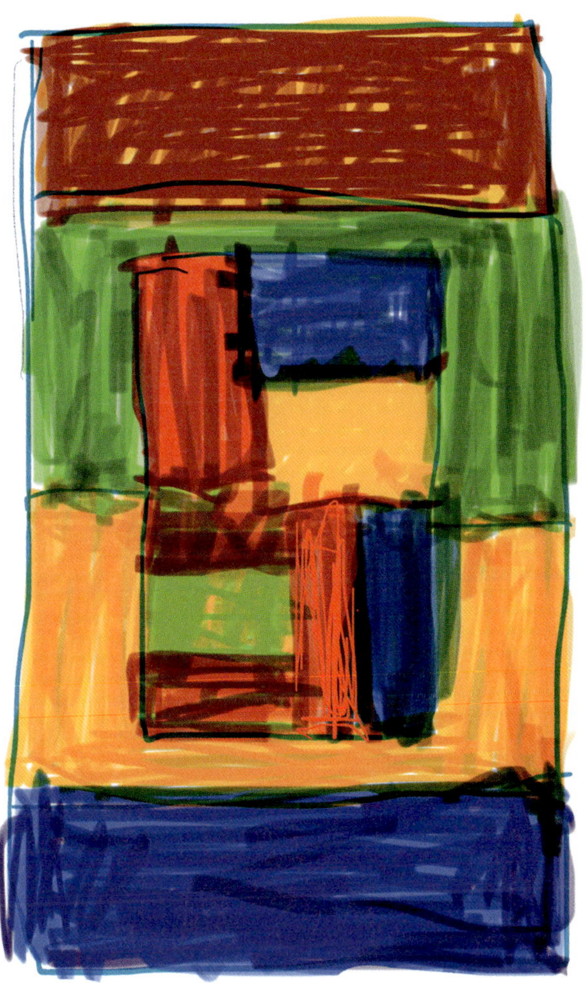

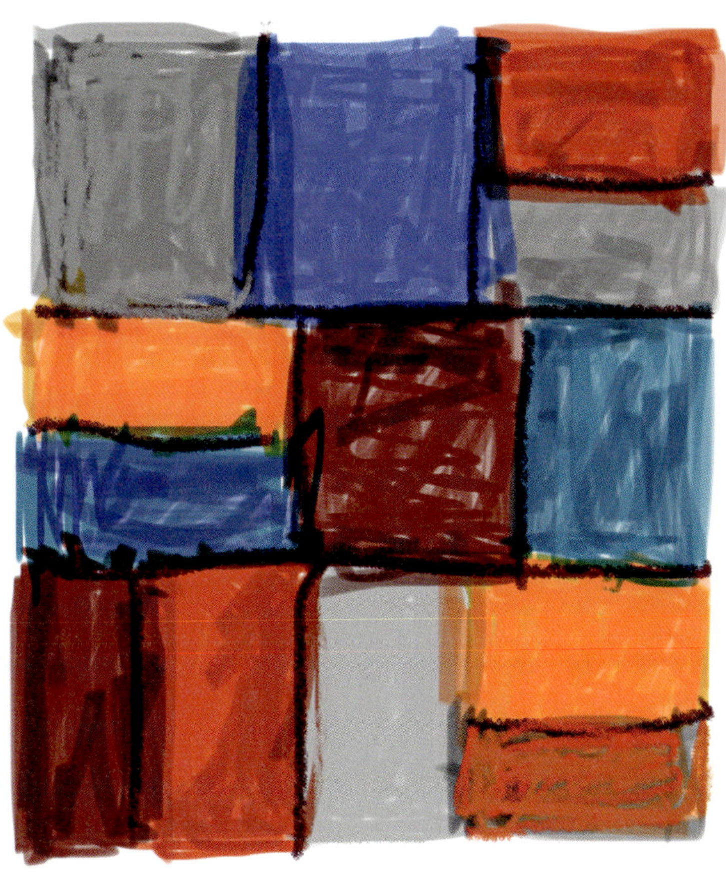

Red-Fronted Macaw

Status: 'Critically endangered' due to pet trade

We are the wires that weave
the cage; we are
the hinge that
time rusts
shut;

we are the shadow of
unstretched wings,
until, my soul,
we've said
enough.

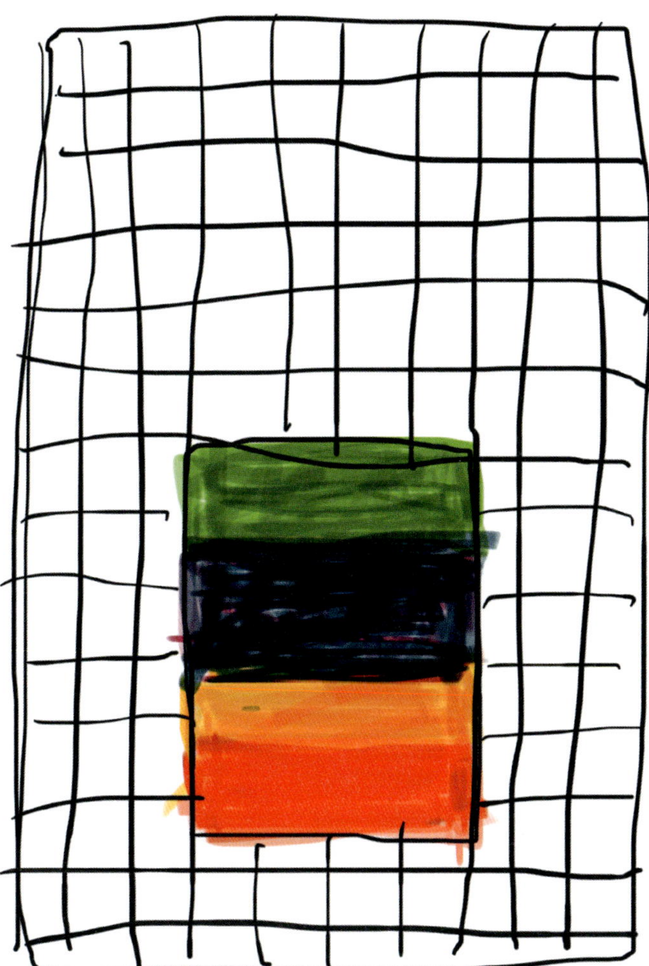

Blue Swallow

Status: 'Vulnerable' due to habitat loss

for Sinéad

A flex of flame before the weightless
plunge of sharpened keel, love
is swifter than the blue
swallow's eye,
lighter

than the lift of rivermist and sweeter
than a fleck of firedusk
falling, falling, falling
on breathsprung
wings.

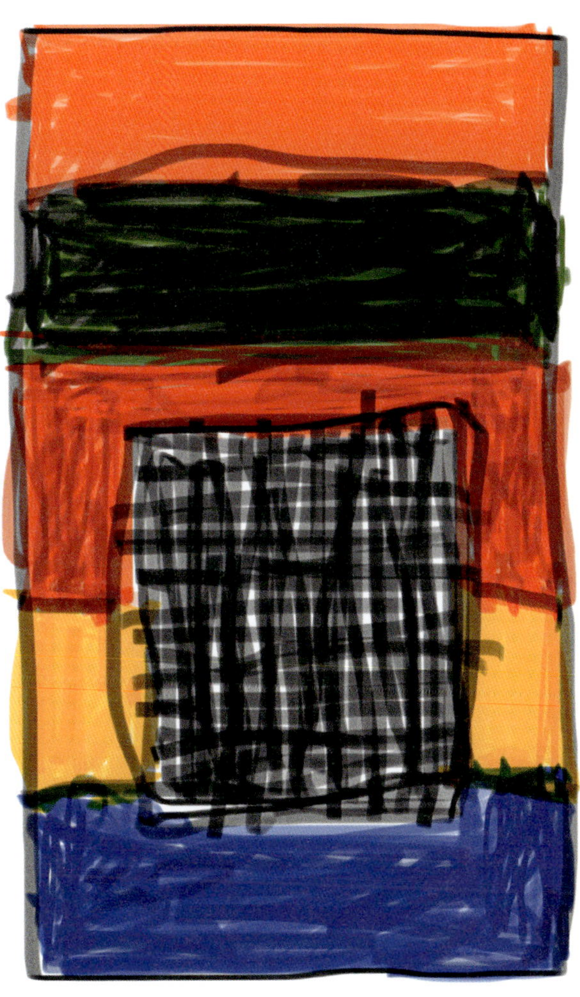

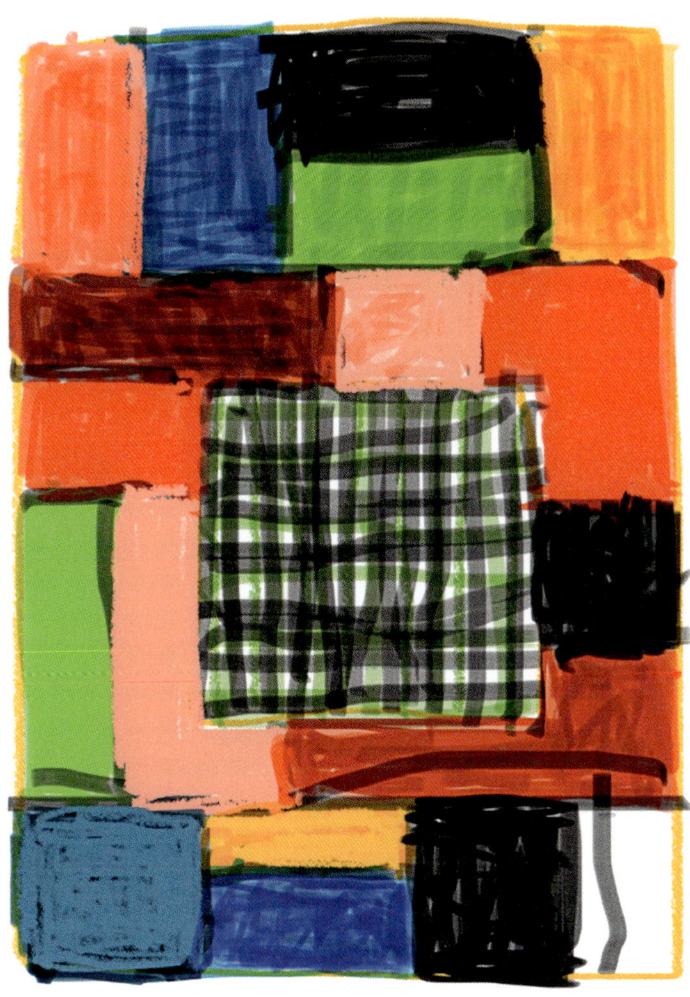

Vows
for Liliane and Sean

Like the echoing flash
of a kingfisher's eye
alighting for a blink
on a babble-
swooped

branch, this moment –
a luminous fin
plucked from
the surge –
whittles

time down to
all time's
timeless
point:
love.

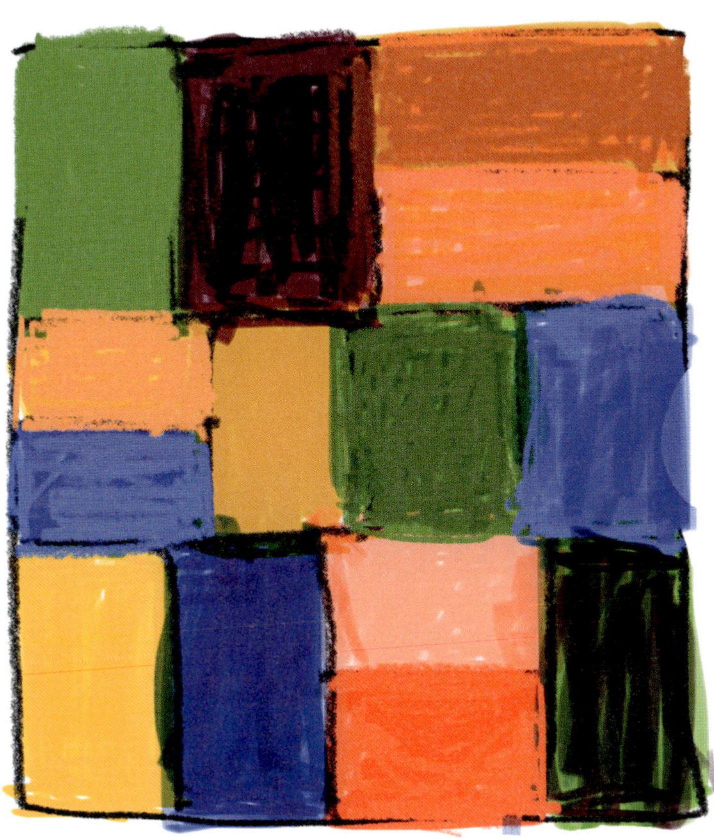

MIT
MEINEM
FINGER

Sean

All the drawings in this book were made by
Sean Scully on an iPhone using the Notes
application over the course of 2021.

BIOGRAPHIES

SEAN SCULLY

Sean Scully was born in Dublin, Ireland, in 1945 and today lives and works between New York, Bavaria, Aix-en-Provence and London.

Sean Scully's work is in the collection of virtually every major museum around the world. In 2014, he became the only Western artist to have had a career-length retrospective exhibition in China. This led to his being awarded the International Artist of the Year Prize in Hong Kong in 2018.

2018–19 also saw important solo exhibitions such as *Landline* at the Hirshhorn Museum and Sculpture Garden in Washington, DC, which toured to the Wadsworth Atheneum, Connecticut, United States; *Landline and Other Works* at the De Pont Museum in the Netherlands; a retrospective titled *Vita Duplex* at the Staatliche Kunsthalle Karlsruhe, Germany; *Sea Star* at the National Gallery, London, and *Inside Outside* the first major exhibition of Sean Scully's sculptures at the Yorkshire Sculpture Park, United Kingdom. *Eleuthera*, Sean Scully's new figurative paintings, were given a solo exhibition at the Albertina, Vienna; the retrospective *Long Light* opened at the Villa and Collection Panza, Varese, Italy; and *HUMAN*, an exhibition of new paintings and sculpture was shown at San Giorgio Maggiore in Venice, Italy, for the 58th Venice Art Biennale.

In 2020, the Hungarian National Gallery, Budapest, opened *Passenger*, a major retrospective and his first exhibition in Central Europe, which travelled to the Benaki Museum, Athens, and the Museum of Contemporary Art, Zagreb, Croatia.

2022 was marked by the major fifty-year career retrospective *Sean Scully: The Shape of Ideas* at the Philadelphia Museum of Art, in Pennsylvania, United States, previously shown at the Modern Art Museum of Fort Worth, Texas, in 2021, alongside three further retrospectives: *Song of Color* at the Langen Foundation, Neuss, Germany; *Painting and Sculpture*, at the Centrum Sztuki Współczesnej (CSW), Toruń, Poland; *A Wound in a Dance with Love*, MAMbo – Museum of Modern Art of Bologna, Italy; and a further important solo exhibition *Material World*, at the Thorvaldsens Museum, Copenhagen, Denmark.

In 2023, Sean Scully's work will be seen in solo exhibitions at Houghton Hall, Norfolk, United Kingdom; Passerelle Centre d'art contemporain, Brest, France; and the He Art Museum, Guangdong, China.

KELLY GROVIER

Kelly Grovier grew up in California and was educated at University of California, Los Angeles and at Oxford University, where he received his doctorate in English literature. He is the author of ten books, including the bestselling survey *A New Way of Seeing: The History of Art in 57 Works* and *On the Line: Conversations with Sean Scully*, both published by Thames & Hudson. He is the author of three collections of poetry with Carcanet Press and is co-founder of the international scholarly journal *European Romantic Review*. He is a feature writer for BBC Culture and his writings on art have appeared in *The Times Literary Supplement*, *The Independent*, *The Sunday Times*, *The Observer*, *RA Magazine* and *Wired* magazine. His most recent book, *The Art of Colour: The History of Art in 39 Pigments* will be published in spring 2023. He lives in Ireland with his wife and son.

COLOPHON

Endangered Sky
Sean Scully & Kelly Grovier

Project management
Adam Jackman

Copy-editing
Aaron Bogart

Graphic design
Neil Holt

Typeface
Scala Pro

Production
Kati Klaeske

Reproductions
Repromayer Medienproduktion GmbH,
Reutlingen

Printing
Livonia Print, Riga

Paper
Arctic Volume White, 130 g/m²

© 2023 Hatje Cantz Verlag, Berlin,
and the author
© 2023 for the reproduced works
by Sean Scully: the artist
© 2023 for the text: Kelly Grovier

In addition to this book, which has
been sponsored by Sean Scully and to
which Kelly Grovier has gifted his
poems, a series of prints have been
made of which 100% of the profits
will be donated to Birdlife International
to support their critical work in
conservation.

Published by
Hatje Cantz Verlag GmbH
Mommsenstraße 27
10629 Berlin
www.hatjecantz.com
A Ganske Publishing Group Company

Trade edition:
ISBN 978-3-7757-5485-9
Special edition:
ISBN 978-3-7757-5505-4

Printed in Europe